Testimonials from Industry Experts

A refreshing and novel take on value investing. An insightful way to look at asset allocation, country allocation and allocation in different sector and stocks.

– **Jimmy Mahtani,** Managing Director,
Barings Private Equity Asia

Most people look at investing into stock markets as day trading, speculation or long term investing – buy and hold forever. In this book Aaditya introduces readers to the Polycycle Investment style with real life examples on how to make money through active investment.

– **Srinivas Rao Ravuri,** Chief Investment Officer – Equities,
PGIM India Mutual Fund

The book looks to break multiple myths related to investing and through real examples from history, talks about how stock picking can be simplified.

– **Mayank Bansal,** Principal,
Global Infrastructure Partners

A very well-written and interesting read for every individual investing in financial markets whether as career professional or portfolio investor, as the book guides you on some very basis as well as fundamental principles of investing, and which you should know as guiding factors. These, too, are always evolving and never static. That message through the book is very well articulated by Aaditya.

– **Yogesh Kapur,** Managing Director,
Axis Capital Ltd.

I found the book very interesting – Aaditya articulates well that 'timing the market' for an active investor is as important, if not more, than 'time in the market'. Aaditya's well-researched examples from the Indian context bring this central point home, and provide a barometer to an active investor looking to invest through multiple cycles in an increasingly volatile world. This books narrates various types of cycles, be it market, commodity, product or currency, and provides perspective on how to continue to be a part of the growth journey in the Indian equities market, while making active and prudent capital allocation decisions. A must-read for investors looking to charter through the India growth story over the next few decades.

– **Nawal Saini,** Managing Director,
Brookfield Asset Management

The Polycycle Investor is a lucidly written collection of true life investing insights gathered by Aaditya in his investment banking career. Throughout the book, his keen observation, honest analysis comes across. He manages to put together numerous real life examples and yet keep together a flow which makes it easy to understand even for an amateur investor. A strong recommendation for the entire investing community.

– **Vivek Chhachhi,** Partner,
CX Partners

Aaditya has a very lucid style of writing and has beautifully brought out the opportunity that investors have as they invest in equity in Indian companies. The book brings out the interplay of various cycles that impact equity investment that an investor needs to bear in mind, and both, protect against as well as use to his advantage. The examples and anecdotes shared make for interesting reading and provide good insights into Indian corporate history and developments. A must-read for all those who want to benefit from the large wealth creation opportunity – the opportunity that Indian equities offer while protecting one's portfolio from the attendant pitfalls and risks.

– **Pankaj Jaju,** Founder,
Metta Capital

An Alternative School of Value Investing

THE POLYCYCLE INVESTOR

AADITYA GUTGUTIA

MANJUL

Manjul Publishing House

First published in India by

MANJUL

Manjul Publishing House

• C-16, Sector 3, Noida, Uttar Pradesh 201301, India
Website: www.manjulindia.com

Registered Office:

• 10, Nishat Colony, Bhopal 462 003 – India

Distribution Centres:

Ahmedabad, Bengaluru, Bhopal, Kolkata, Chennai, Hyderabad, Mumbai, New Delhi, Pune

This edition first published in 2021
Second impression 2022

ISBN 978-93-90924-96-7

Printed and bound in India by Thomson Press (India) Ltd.

Contents

Acknowledgements

The fundamental ideas for this book have been rolling in my head for a few years but like all good things, they took their own sweet time to finally get written. The lockdown because of Covid-19 and the resulting free time had me putting my thoughts together.

This journey of penning my experiences in the capital markets could never have been possible without the role my gurus played in my life. Prof. Sanjay Bakshi sowed the initial seeds of love for value-investing and for reading relatively early in my life; he kindled my love for stocks and to be able to see the businesses behind these stocks.

I would also like to thank Yogesh Kapur and Ambrish Singh, who gave me my first investment banking job and the opportunity to learn about businesses from the best professionals and owners of various businesses. They continue to be my mentors and guides, and I am extremely grateful for their guidance during the course of my career.

I have been extremely fortunate to work under the tutelage of some best in-class professionals like Manish Chokhani, Gautam Jain, Dr. Subramanian, Vikas Khemani, Nilesh Shah and Pankaj Jaju, each of them an institution in themselves, greatly enriching my education in the nuances of various businesses and industries.

The journey could not have been so exciting and fulfilling without my clients who trusted me for advice or for raising capital, and in the process spent time to help me learn the intricacies of the businesses they run. Similarly, the investors who spent time on various investing opportunities have also contributed immensely in helping me understand risks associated with businesses.

I would also like to thank friends Nikhil Arora, Mayank Bansal and Ravi Kumar Kesavan, who helped me in writing this book with invaluable inputs on editing and publishing.

Last but not the least, my family members: my brother Neeraj, who guided me through the entire process and consistently helped with direction and micro-level inputs on the book; my wife Kajal, who was a pillar of support during these times and helped immensely with creatives and the look and feel of the book and the website. Also, my parents, who have always been the inspiration and source of strength for everything I do – I am sure their blessings will make this endeavour successful too.

Foreword

When I first received the request from Aaditya to write the foreword for the book, the first thing I was curious about was: how different is it from so much of the literature that is already out there on the subject by various writers. What got me interested to do this was the Indian context to the book and the real-life examples used in the book. While there are enough and more instructive books, as well as books about the value creators in India, I thought this book had a very novel and persuasive way of approaching the doctrine of investing in India.

Most investment professionals are conscious of the cycles that affect individual companies. However, the ability to weave that understanding into your capital allocation strategy in practice is a very difficult art. I am sure this book will help both amateur and professional investors devise their own strategies to allocate capital across cycles.

I have always maintained that professional investors in India have consistently outclassed the best in class investors globally over a sustained period of time. I have personally had the pleasure of working with some of the top professionals in the space who have consistently outclassed their more illustrious global counterparts. While there is no denying the skills our professionals possess, some of the success is also attributable to the fact that India as a country is going through a metamorphosis that is creating tremendous value for businesses, investors and the economy as a whole.

While the past three decades have created tremendous value, I do feel the best time for an Indian investor and the Indian capital markets is yet to come. India has been consistently treated unfairly by global credit-rating agencies. India has a track record of no default for over 5,000 years, is growing rapidly, has a better external debt to GDP ratio than most other large economies, has a rich culture of household savings, and yet gets a rating just a notch above junk grade. Honestly, I find it laughable.

One would think in a globally expansionary world, India's fiscal prudence will force the hands of the rating agencies to correct that, and global capital will find it increasingly more difficult to extort disproportionately high returns by hiding behind these absurd credit ratings.

India's reducing cost of capital coupled with demography, entrepreneurial spirit and its culture of savings will create opportunities and wealth for investors like never before. To that extent I do second Aaditya's opinion that India is truly 'A Polycycle Bonanza' for investors who can identify the right themes to bet on.

This book is also important because it captures the country's capital market history from an investor's perspective and explains the state of economy and various sectors on a point-of-time basis, and I hope this helps create even more interesting literature and language around investing that is India-centric. Wishing Aaditya all success with the book! I am sure the readers will like the narrative as much as I did.

Nilesh Shah

Mr. Nilesh Shah is one of the most sought-after thought leaders in India's capital market history. Currently, Mr. Shah is the managing director of Kotak Mahindra Asset Management Co Ltd. He has over 25 years of experience in capital markets and market-related investments, having managed funds across equity, fixed-income securities and real estate for local and global investors.

Preface

The wheels of the cycles are a-moving!

Any complex economy is like wheels within wheels, cycles within cycles. Like a Swiss clock with many wheels running its different hands, each wheel plays a role to make sure one does not lose or gain time. Similarly, a complex economy, whether global or national, has many such wheels. Stakeholders in the economy are impacted by these cycles.

For an investor, an understanding of these cycles is probably the single-most important tool. This is one of the most underrated and probably the least talked about skill in the investing fraternity. We often hear refrains like 'one cannot time the market', 'time in the market is more important than timing the market', 'quality stocks always deliver superior returns'. Some of these maxims have made more and more value investors look alike.

In 2019, we were living in a bubble for quality stocks. Some of the winners of the past decade will find it impossible to sustain those kinds of multiples for a very long time, especially given that some of these 'quality' stocks are in sectors being disrupted, leading to a loss in market share, margins, disintermediation and technological change.

The book is an attempt to help investors identify these cycles and make appropriate capital allocation decisions, including the virtue of having cash when the opportunity presents itself. This also gives an investor tools to identify market excesses and sector excesses in order to get allocation within sectors and stocks right.

The contents are designed to help the reader find new mental models to help identify themes and stocks that can create long-term value for their portfolio by playing cycles. From here on we will call an investor who is a student of playing these multiple interplays of cycles as a Polycycle Investor.

When we think of cycles, we assume all are round, but some are not. Not everything that goes down will come up; some will go down further till they hit the abyss and then go down some more. Insolvencies, bankruptcies, permanent decline of capital and industries will become more and more commonplace in the coming decade. Hence, it is important to understand these various cycles and the threats they pose to portfolio returns.

Another variable that has had an unimaginable impact on the pace of change in the last two decades has been the easy availability of equity capital to fund aggregation and disintermediation businesses, making smaller businesses in these spaces redundant. Online travel portals have made the neighbourhood travel agent redundant, big e-commerce giants have made a large number of retail formats irrelevant, players like Lenskart are making the optical store next-door sweat. The online distribution of insurance and mutual funds and the plethora of advice available not only hurt the commissions of financial advisors, but also make a dent in the profits of larger intermediaries. Ola and Uber are ensuring closure of neighbourhood taxi stands. Even Mastercard and Visa are facing the heat from falling merchant fee in a space that was largely a duopoly and at best an oligopoly for decades. The examples are dime a dozen.

These business models are causing large-scale disruptions. But what is equally important to understand is that these disruptions are creating a huge consumer surplus with better quality advice, understanding and lower costs. An average middle-class consumer today is a lot more tech-savvy, finance-savvy, social media-savvy and knowledgeable about tools of efficient price discovery for the product they want to buy or services they wish to use. That advice for all this is available at a click clearly helps.

I hope that the lessons in this book, which I have tried to elucidate with live and often personal examples, will be a heady ride and enrich your investing experience. So, let's time the market!

Aaditya Gutgutia

1

Timing the Market

Most of behavioural finance and security analysis literature talks about the virtue of 'time in the market' as against 'timing the market'. However, if one looks at investing as a multi-decade activity, investors will shoot up their CAGR[1] (compound annual growth rate) significantly once they learn when to enter and exit a stock and also when to reduce and increase capital allocation of the portfolio to stocks.

The rate of change in the world is increasing, and the impact of geo-political tensions and actions of large states on global economy is more pronounced than ever. The world has seen a cold war between the two superpowers from the 1960s to the 1980s, where the machinations of the two superpowers had a bearing on the political fortunes of other nations.

Probably the world has entered another cold-war era with the United States and China being at the forefront of the global geo-strategic tensions. Only this time the world economies are much more globalized, more currencies are free float, and probably the importance of stability in the US dollar is more pronounced for the global economy than ever before. Amidst all this, the United States

1. Compound Annual Growth Rate also means annualized return. The term will be used fairly often and interchangeably during the course of the book.

has been ratcheting up huge budget deficits, making the global currency markets nervous.

At the same time, rapid changes in technology, the use of new digital platforms, and the rise of big tech firms like Google, Amazon, Facebook and Apple are disrupting the old business order at an unprecedented rate. Technology is not only disrupting businesses you invest in, but algorithm-based trading is also disrupting the business of investing dramatically. In such a dynamic environment, it has become an absolute must to be able to time your entry and exit in/from an individual stock and the market. Let us look at some examples across various cycles on why timing your investments is an absolute must.

Market cycles and frontrunners of market cycles

Getting the timing right in allocating your money to the markets is one of the greatest value creators. Being able to take money off the table not only saves one from years of underperformance, but also gives liquidity to invest and buy larger quantities of stocks in an adverse market.

Timing the market, to that extent, is not an exercise in trying to catch the top or the bottom of a stock in the short run. This is a more deliberate exercise to better understand the business cycle and the market cycle, and find signs to decide when to exit an individual stock or the market in general.

An investor who can reduce a significant bit of allocation to stock markets near the peak of a bull run and further increase allocations when markets start to come off, progressively, will make a far superior return on his portfolio over a longer run than a very smart and clever stock picker. Investing is as much an art of capital allocation as it is an art of stock picking.

The 2008 global financial crisis (GFC) to that extent was a multi-cycle wave climaxing together, creating a perfect storm or tsunami, leaving a widespread trail of disaster across asset classes and investors. Financial services, commodities, stock markets, real estate and almost every asset class were getting increasingly expensive, buoyed by the super credit cycle being created worldwide, and the 'wealth effect' further fueling the consumption, tourism and asset ownership boom. The crash was only a matter of time.

One of the asset classes in an unprecedented boom across the world and also in India was real estate. The real estate industry witnessed a large capital raising cycle, with PE investors, capital markets and all other classes of investors keen to participate in the sector. Promoters and senior executives of real estate companies were themselves sold on the stories they were telling the market, and started creating large land banks that could not be consumed even in multiple decades. Access to cheaper capital and buoyancy in capital markets made everyone believe that the party would never stop.

Since 2008, probably real estate stocks have been the biggest value destroyer with asset values stagnating, capital costs increasing and corporate governance issues in many of the real estate companies coming to fore.

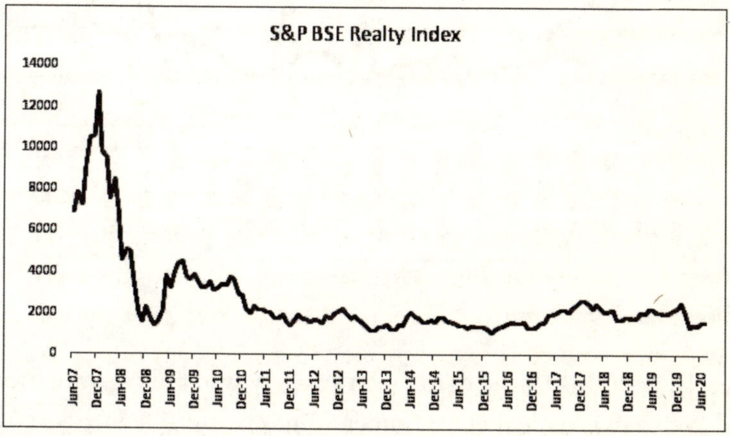

Source: BSE

No matter how diligent you were, if you bit into the real estate super cycle and follies attached with it, irrespective of your stock pick, you would have lost money in the market or made very little returns; and even after the initial collapse you would be sitting with stocks in a sector with little or negative returns for a decade. Even a late entrant into the sector who exited after the crash, acknowledging that the sector was fundamentally damaged, would have been better off than an investor who would have looked to cling to his 'undervalued' or 'quality' real estate stocks.

One of the most striking examples of how timing the market can have an impact on your portfolio returns is Infosys. If you entered Infosys at the beginning of fiscal 2001 and exited towards the end of fiscal 2005 you would have made zero returns on the stock. This in a time, when the company's performance and growth were superlative.

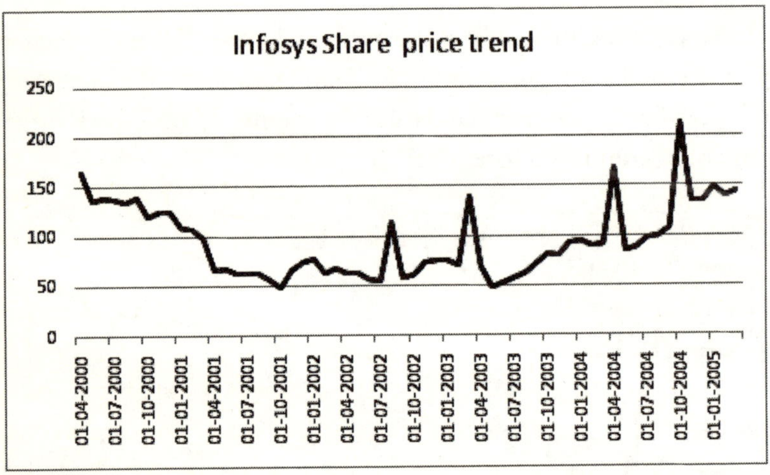

Infosys share price trend

Clearly, in 2000-01, the entire tech space was in bubble valuations, and even a market leader and super-value creator like Infosys could not have given any returns to its stockholders if someone would have chosen to buy that stock in the middle of the tech boom. The PAT (profit after tax) of Infosys went from INR 293.5 crores to

INR 1,891 crores in these five years. Imagine profitability going 6X in 5 years with no capital appreciation.

Needless to add, Infosys has been a torchbearer for value creation, corporate governance and performance for multiple decades. But there is no way one can make money on top of a market bubble, especially if that sector is the engine behind the froth.

While Infosys went on to create tremendous shareholder value post-2005, some of the other engines following bull markets like real estate in 2007 did not do so. One would think NBFCs (non-banking finance companies), which were a darling of the markets till 2018 before the IL&FS crisis happened, will not be able to replicate the success of Infosys either.

The key difference between Infosys in the tech bubble and real estate in 2008 or NBFCs in 2018 is leverage. Leverage is a reverse compounding machine in adverse times that damages balance sheets beyond recognition. A protracted reverse compounding can make even perfectly good and efficient businesses go into permanent decline. Further, both these businesses are also consumer confidence businesses. If the trust in a real estate company or in the sector overall is impacted, consumers are more and more reluctant to buy from them.

Similarly, if the trust on the balance sheet of an NBFC or a bank decreases to a point where the broader market starts doubting its ability to pay back, the cost of capital increases disproportionately, and they find it impossible to lend in a profitable manner without being out-priced by competitors with stronger balance sheets and access to cheaper capital. This is why post-IL&FS crisis, a lot of NBFCs are headed for an irreversible decline. At the time of writing, DHFL and Yes Bank had already gone bankrupt and some of the other NBFCs like Edelweiss, Indiabulls and Piramal have corrected anywhere between 60% to 90% from their peaks.

While the stock prices, with right interventions and equity raise, may partially retrace over a period of time, the damage done to their ability to raise cheap capital may be more long drawn or even permanent in nature.

Timing and commodity cycles

The importance of timing in commodity cycles is probably the easiest to understand theoretically, but the most difficult to play. Easy availability of credit and the ability to raise equity capital encourage companies to take risks and bets they would never take in a more conservative environment.

In 2007, Tatas acquired a disproportionately larger steel behemoth Corus and paid $11 billion for an 18 MnTPA (million tonnes per annum) plant. According to a Macquarie research report of those times, the asset was valued at $480 per tonne against $700 per tonne that Tatas paid. Even DSP Merrill Lynch had pegged the valuation at a similar range. The EV/EBITDA paid for the acquisition was 9x, which is kind of unheard of in the commodity space, and that too in a moderate-to-flat growth European market. Just as a benchmark, Mittals paid 4.6x of historic EBITDA to acquire Arcelor. *(Source: The Indian Express, Feb 1/2007).*

One also needs to appreciate that steel itself was on an upcycle in 2007, so the assets seemed to be valued significantly above replacement value. If one couples this with the cocktail of high leverage to do the buy-out, the impact on shareholders of Tata Steel was devastating. Tata Steel, which used to trade above INR 400 for most of 2007, after 13 years still trades at INR 275 per share in 2020. They lost domestic market share to JSW Steel and Jindal Steel and some of the other large competitors. However, now they are looking to make up for some of those by acquiring domestic steel assets under the Insolvency and Bankruptcy Code. The market leader in steel, with decades of understanding of the commodity and its cycles, fell prey to a concoction of commodity upcycle and super credit cycle, and combined leverage to pay a heavy price for the same.

The oldest kind of commodity cycles is the one seen in agriculture and foodgrains. Typically, these cycles were 2-3 years' cycles. In one year, because of a lesser production in one particular crop (say A), the price of that crop would go up, encouraging other farmers to move from a lower priced crop (say B) to the one that is priced higher. In the following year, this behaviour would lead to lesser production of crop B and higher production of crop A, leading to a fall in price of crop A and increase in price of B. The government took care of some of these cyclical vagaries to ensure food security by promising a minimum support price for essential crops.

However, government incentives and price support started creating a different kind of a problem, especially where the crop was being bought by private players and not by the government. Yes, we are talking about sugarcane. In 2004, on the back of a weaker production sugar prices were at an all-time high. The difference between the selling price and state-advised price (SAP) of sugarcane in the state of Uttar Pradesh (UP) was generating super normal profits for sugar mill-owners.

In addition was a scheme called Sugar Development Fund (SDF), which gave cheap loans to sugar manufacturers. Further, the UP government in 2004 came out with a 10% capital subsidy for setting up new sugar mills. This virtually meant that a lot of sugar players were able to plan large capacity expansions without having to put in too much upfront equity and having a relatively manageable interest burden. What could have gone wrong? Well, everything! According to estimates, the industry added 2,84,000 TCD (tonnes crushing per day) in the post-policy period with a cumulative capex (capital expenditure) of over INR 7,400 crores in UP alone.

This led to a glut in sugar production; to make matters worse, the state government increased the SAP to INR 280 per quintal, and the new incoming government scrapped the capital subsidy policy. This was the perfect storm for the UP sugar mills, causing losses, unpaid cane due to farmers and a prolonged period of under-utilization of capacities and debt restructuring.

It might have still made sense from the perspective of owners of these businesses to maintain their market share, increase capacities and do what is needed, but if minority shareholders see too much capacity building up in a commodity sector, it is time to take money home.

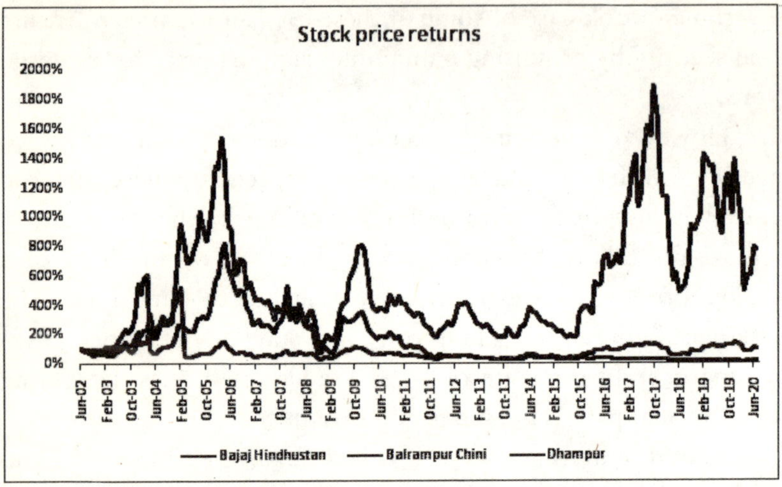

So, whether you bought into market leaders or laggards, it was virtually impossible to make money in a super-cycle like that, especially where the raw material price was controlled by the government, while the end-produce price was largely market-driven. To recognize the cycle and exit in time was important. That's not to say money was not made. Between 2003 and 2005, investors in the space made crazy returns.

Basmati players in India also went through a cycle where they made lots of money, leading to increased capacities and then evaporation of margins and players. More on the basmati rice industry later.

If apart from the debt in a company's balance sheet, a stock market investor had invested in these stocks by taking debts on his own balance sheet, he would have lost staying power and would have caused permanent damage to his portfolios. Hence, it is extremely important that the old-school wisdom of avoiding leverage while investing and diversification of portfolio, both in terms of stocks and sectors, is not overlooked.

Large capex and high-operating leverage businesses

Indian telecom players went through the same cycle. Bharti Airtel, probably the lone survivor from the previous decade, reached its 2007 share price only in 2019. Imagine 12 years of virtually no returns. Every other player in the space went belly up, destroying unimaginable shareholder wealth.

This is when the tele-density in India in 2007 was 20.6 crores telephone subscribers (mobile and landline), while it increased to 121.1 crores subscribers by end of 2019. Imagine over a 12-year period tele-density becomes almost 6x, the number of players come down dramatically, and the only large significant player to survive in the space does not grow its per share value.

The story of Bharti Airtel is different from some of the other examples discussed earlier. It is a classic problem of being in an industry where a large part of the capex is upfront, requires repeated re-investments, but the end price is determined by competition and end consumers. This is somewhat similar to the airline industry, with an additional challenge of needing continuous and large additional capex, technology upgrade and spectrum purchases.

The airline industry has a slightly different challenge: there is capex, and then there is a long period of large customer acquisition costs, where you need to run an airline on losses to build a network and improve your fleet utilization, brand, pricing power and limited control on end pricing. Around 2000, two of the most enterprising airline companies that changed the face of private aviation in India, Air Deccan and Kingfisher, went through the same cycle and eventually were either sold off or went bankrupt before being able to make significant profits to justify the same.

One feels that a lot of the e-commerce models of today work on the same premises as starting an airline around 2000. There is a period of brand-building, there is a further period of large customer acquisition costs to get economies of scale and network benefits, but the end price continues to be market-driven. Airlines at least had airline leases, airport slots and a large pool of fixed assets; these e-commerce models don't have much. Unless one is able to cross the required threshold and achieve the required scale and network benefits, the e-commerce models are very difficult to make money from.

A Polycycle Investor would do well to stay away from businesses models like airlines and loss-making e-commerce companies most of the time. One may think of missing out on an opportunity to buy players like Amazon, or Info Edge in the Indian context when they were young, but the graveyard of e-commerce companies is replete with names that have fallen by the way without a trace or a fighting chance. Though the Indian e-commerce market is still evolving, one cannot forget names like Snapdeal, Myntra, Zivame, Jabong, ShopClues. These are still names one remembers and managed to get multiple rounds of fund raising – some of them got sold to worthy suitors also. But for every such name, there are grocery retailers like AskMeGrocery and GrocerMax, apparel retailers like yebhi.com and hundreds of others that have faded from our collective memory.

Investing in these businesses at an early stage is often like buying a lottery ticket, hoping one of the many tickets will be the winning one. However, the view on some of these changes the moment they reach a domain, where cash flows from the business exceed their client acquisition cost. Further, if they are playing in a domain which has a niche, where industry size is large enough to give them a long runway but not large enough for Mr. Moneybags to want to come and disrupt the space by burning more and more cash, they become investible businesses. Similarly, the larger evolved businesses, able to flank their competitive positions, also become investible.

Another very interesting example of timing in a high-operating leverage business is the movies exhibition business. Let us look at how timing your purchase in this business can impact your returns. Mr. X is an excellent stock picker and his favourite holding period is forever. He invested in PVR Cinemas on 27th July 2015 at INR 843 per share. It was a great pick and the stock went up 2.5 times in the next four years. Then the pandemic struck, the business got the jolt of a lifetime and now he has no return to show for such a fantastic pick. He still believes that it is a great quality company and continues to hold on.

Mr. Y, a Polycycle Investor, had bought the same stock in the 2008 crash, when it was trading around INR 100 a share, business was still fantastic, growth rates were good, and at least in the NCR (National Capital Region, which includes Delhi and adjacent townships like Gurugram and Noida) it was a market leader. He understood the market cycle and deployed larger pools of cash. When the coronavirus fear started spreading, he understood the import, but by the time he could sell, the stock had already come down from the peak of INR 2,000 to INR 1,500. He still made 15x over a period of 12 years. He not only understood the turning market cycle effectively, he also understood that with the advent of OTT platforms like Netflix, Prime Video, Zee5, and multiple such high-quality platforms coupled with increased penetration of broadband, the industry itself would be in a secular decline. There was no way he was willing to hold on to a stock in the middle of a disaster and in an industry that can potentially de-grow at multiples of 35x P/E.

Both Mr. X and Mr. Y believe that this is an excellent consumer-facing company and picked the stock probably at the right time according to them. The only difference was Mr. Y played the market cycle, Covid-19 disruption and industry cycle better. That in the end made all the difference.

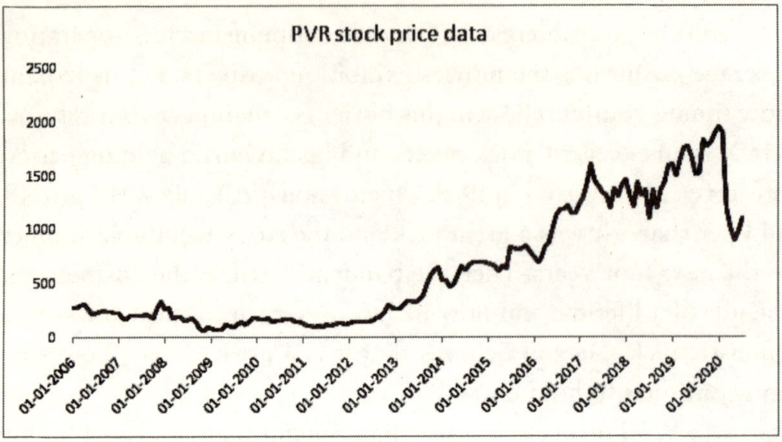

Timing the market may look like hindsight bias at best and voodoo at worst to many market players. But there is research, keen understanding and a longer term temperament to look at investing as a multi-decade activity which allows an investor to identify these patterns in a more lucid manner.

Capital allocation and leverage

While being completely out or being unduly levered to invest are both risky and undesirable propositions, capital allocation decisions to play the market can have disproportionate benefits for an investor. Investing in cycles has its own risks, and one should be willing to take some losses, but as an investor you do not wish to lose money when you are right. Leverage often does that to even high-quality investments.

The most important risk for a Polycycle Investor is leverage. He has to be extremely cautious of leverage not only in his stock picks but also his personal leverage. He neither wants his pick to go bankrupt before the cycle turns, nor does he want to be in a situation of having to sell his position in the stock because his personal leverage is unsustainable. Being conscious of personal leverage is something that needs to be taught in schools, so that from early on students understand the risks of leverage and the impact of negative compounding on their respective future lives.

While it is important to manage leverage, it is also important to have reasonable allocation to high conviction stocks. Mr. X, like we said earlier, is an excellent stock picker and often finds stocks that eventually turn out to be multi-baggers. However, he rarely allocates more than 40% of his investible surplus in stocks, as he likes to diversify into real estate, debt and gold. As a 'prudent investor', he typically diversifies across 20-25 stocks. Two of his picks turn out to be a five-bagger. Some other gave impressive returns, some returned losses. One would have thought that those five-baggers would have made up for everything else. But they constituted only 3% of his investible surplus at the time of investment; the needle on the portfolio returns did not move by much. Over a period of five years, the five-baggers moved the CAGR by only 1.5% or so.

However, Mr. Y, the Polycycle Investor, looks at capital allocation as closely as the stock picks. He allocates up to 150% of his investible surplus in deep bear markets, which he defines as Sensex or Nifty multiples below 14, and only 35% of his investible surplus in bull markets. He also allocates a higher percentage of capital in low-risk high conviction stock and is even happy with owning less than 15 stocks and allocating up to 15% to a single stock. One of his high conviction stocks where he had allocated 15% at the bottom of a cycle turns out to be a five-bagger. Because of moderate leveraging, this allocation of 15% of his equity portfolio to that stock meant allocation of 20% of his investible surplus being allocated to that particular stock. Once a stock like that becomes even a five-bagger, the impact on overall portfolio returns is really significant. The impact of this investment on the portfolio CAGR was as high as 5-6% over a five-year period.

I think most long-term investors understand the power of compounding fairly well, but still the impact of five percentage points on a multi-decade investor's portfolio cannot be over-emphasized. INR 1 lakh invested at a 10% CAGR for 20 years will be worth INR 6,72,750, while INR 1 lakhs invested at 15% CAGR for 20 years will be worth INR 16,36,654. Over a long period of time and with larger sums invested, this difference is potentially life-changing. The more we draw out the timelines, the impact on portfolio growth of this incremental CAGR becomes spectacularly obvious.

This kind of investing style needs a lot of discipline and an understanding of the risks. Leveraging at the top of the cycle could be fatal and can wipe off lifetime earnings in no time. Similarly, when one is looking at a high conviction stock, one has to be cognizant of the product life cycle, leverage and the kind of threats it faces from its competitors and the environment. One must at least feel confident that over a five-year period the business fundamentals of the stock will continue to be robust, and the earnings will not be adversely impacted beyond a point. We will discuss the qualities that one needs to identify to mitigate risks associated with high capital allocation to a high conviction stock later in the book, when we discuss risk mitigation strategies.

Agency risks of recommending de-allocation of capital

Being able to time the market is one of the critical advantages a small investor or a flexible investor has over institutional investors. Institutional investors have two very distinct disadvantages: a) their charter and b) having to report NAV (net asset value) on a daily basis and performance on a monthly or quarterly basis.

The charter of most equity-linked mutual funds restricts and puts a limit on the amount of cash they can hold. Often, the common refrain is that if they can't deploy cash, they should not mobilize it. This is a serious flaw that does not enable them to hold larger pools of cash to deploy when the market turns or the bubble bursts. Fund managers will probably have a very tough time with their CIOs (chief investment officers) if they keep sitting on large pools of cash. Even managers in most portfolio management schemes (PMS) have a similar problem unless they are able to communicate their investing strategies effectively to their clients.

They are always competing with the returns of their peers and new fund mobilization is dependent on their short-term and mid-term portfolio returns, so they need to always be invested in the market. Also, they are chasing returns in stocks likely to give better returns in the short term. They cannot afford to have even two quarters of relative weaker performance due to a larger capital allocation to cash. Further, to demonstrate better quarterly performance, they are more likely to invest in sectors that have the momentum with them, and hence are probably already trading at a premium valuation.

For instance, in the 2018-2020 bull run, there was talk of a bubble building in 'quality' stocks. Most of the large quality FMCG (fast-moving consumer goods) companies like Nestlé, Dabur and Hindustan Unilever were trading at 50x P/E even though the consumption was slowing. Similarly, banking and financial services sector leaders like the HDFC twins and Kotak Mahindra Bank were trading at 4x P/BV, even breaching 6x P/BV at its peak. A moderately growing TCS was trading at 35x P/E. Avenue Supermarts (DMart), another stock market darling, has been trading at over a 100x PE and over 25 times book value since its listing and well into the Covid crisis.

However, fund managers with large SIP (systematic investment plan) inflows and performance pressures continued to invest in these stocks, taking the multiples further up. These are all fantastic and good companies, but as a Polycycle Investor, one would find it very difficult to enter these stocks at such high multiples, especially in the retail sector, which is consistently being threatened worldwide by e-commerce majors. The space in India is super-competitive with two deep-pocketed large e-commerce players in Flipkart (Walmart-owned) and Amazon, and a third deep-pocketed player like Reliance itching to get onto the bandwagon even more aggressively through expansion of physical stores and through online platform JioMart.

I have no doubt that a Polycycle Investor will not only avert some disasters, but will also make far superior returns by avoiding these businesses. In the medium term, there may be some pain of having missed out on returns from obvious quality stocks. There is no harm in paying up for quality, but buying quality at any price can at best be described as laziness and risk-averseness of a professional who is indulging in an agency business. He knows he can be hauled up for a wrong call in a mid-cap stock or if his predictions on a cyclical turn takes longer to play out, but he is very unlikely to be hauled up for investing in large-cap quality stocks, especially if all his peers from other fund houses are also invested in them.

Hence, the advantage an ordinary investor or an investor with a trusted investment advisor has over mutual fund investors is phenomenal. What is also important is the education in terms of how businesses are supposed to play out and learning from your mistakes and those of others while making day to day decisions. Even the best of professionals and organisations managed by very sophisticated promoters often fail to look at cycles in terms of making decisions.

In a nutshell, to make money in equities one has to understand the market cycle, business cycle, product cycle, the nature of the business and the risks associated in terms of financial leverage, operating leverage and competitive dynamics. The good part is that it is not as difficult as it may initially seem. Further, the mathematics is so much in favour of a Polycycle Investor that one is allowed to make more than one investing mistake and still make a lot of money.

A Polycycle Investor is typically looking at multi-baggers over a period of 3-8 years of investing horizon in a particular stock. In a 10-stock portfolio if one can get three five-baggers over an average holding period of five years, the rest of the portfolio returns take care of themselves, even if a couple of calls go wrong.

Also, one of the common mistakes a Polycycle Investor makes and will always make is either over-estimating the immediacy of a cyclical turn or over-estimating the extent of the cyclical turn that may impact return on some of the stocks in his portfolio. However, one seldom goes wrong on both counts. If the cyclical turn takes longer than anticipated, then more often than not the upturn is also more acute. If there is manageable leverage in the books of the portfolio company as well as in own balance sheet, one has the ability to wait. That makes all the difference!

2

Credit Cycle

A credit cycle is like the Titanic – a glorious, big and glamorous ship that looks like one big party when sailing in all its glory – but there is always an iceberg lurking ahead. Once it hits the iceberg, the sea is vast, chilling and unending, and lifeboats are fewer than you need. The only way to be saved is when the government finally decides to send a rescue team.

Privileged guests who can buy their way out are always the first ones to be saved, then come the women and children; the able-bodied strong men are left to fend for themselves. Do we see a parallel with the 2008 GFC? Big banks like Citi, Bank of America and AIG of the world were 'too big to fail' and had to be saved by TARP (Troubled Asset Relief Program). The rest of the businesses and the economy were given further support by printing more currency, the poor going on the dole, while the middle class and workers deal with wage cuts, loss of jobs and loss of capital.

This is probably one of the easiest cycles to identify, but what is not easy to identify is the right time to get out, unless you have your binoculars and can see an iceberg from far. A credit cycle is invariably marked by high asset prices, low interest costs, high wage growth, increasing leverage in corporates and individuals alike. This leveraging leads to a heightened level of economic activity, often not backed by any real underlying demand.

The global financial crisis of 2008

Across all major economies, GFC saw a secular rise in real estate prices, fall in interest rates and high wage growth. Lower interest and availability of equity capital fired the animal spirits of entrepreneurs looking to expand their businesses and increase asset ownership. Real estate, which was one of the favoured sectors of providers of capital, saw an unprecedented fervour of activity. The construction and property building activity was such that many major economies even today have excess real estate supply that has not been absorbed more than a decade later.

The crash not only broke the balance sheet of real estate players, but also broke the balance sheet of providers of capital to the space. Large banks like Lehman Brothers and Bear Stearns went belly up, and more than a dozen others had to be bailed out. The unemployment rate in the US increased from 4.4% at the end of 2006 to 9.9% in 2009 and went back to its old levels only by 2017.

Much of the global literature on GFC is US-centric but what happened with some of the other countries like Ireland, hailed as the Celtic Tiger in the 2000s for its economic growth model, is even more heartrending. The Ireland Stock Exchange Overall Index (ISEQ) fell from a high of nearly 10,000 at its peak to 2,000, and in 2020, even after 12 years, the ISEQ is still south of 6,000. Ireland now finds itself bracketed in the unflattering PIIGS (Portugal, Italy, Ireland, Greece and Spain) club of economies, which are seen as fragile with very high debt-to-GDP ratio. The unemployment rate went up from 4.98% in 2007 to 15.45% in 2012 *(source: macrotrends.net)*. The entire country continued to reel under negative to zero growth rate all the way up to 2014.

The global financial crisis within itself had multiple upcycles in real estate, commodities, crude and financial services. Resource owners and mining companies were in a commodity price frenzy fueled by hot money chasing more and more asset ownership. When the prices were continuously going up, there was a huge left-out feeling among those sitting with liquidity, a feeling that they were falling behind in the race for wealth creation. Wealth creation looked easy. Clearly, this couldn't have ended well.

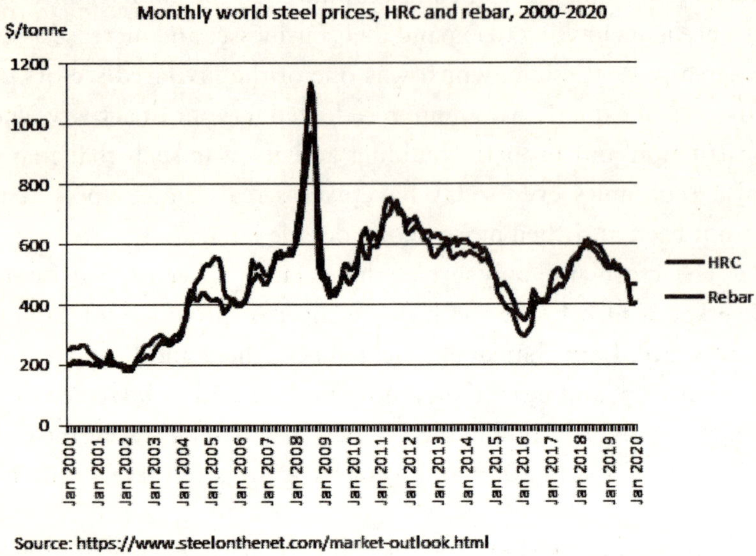

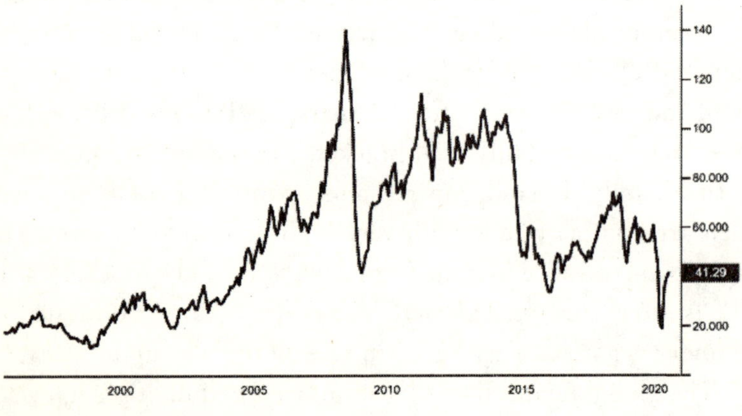

Source: tradingecoonomics.com; Brent crude price trend

In hindsight, it might look obvious that smart money should not be chasing asset ownership in this environment, but all forms of money, smart and otherwise, were chasing asset ownership without worrying if there was a commensurate usage or ownership demand.

Thanks to the US dollar's status as the reserve currency of the world, and its ability to continue to finance its increasing budgetary deficits and an adverse balance of trade through printing more currency, they could refinance the holes in their balance sheets by printing more and more currency and bringing back a semblance of demand in the global markets. More about this and what happened with other currencies later.

A similar crisis happened in 1997 with the Asian Tiger economies, which had seen rapid industrialization in the preceding years, fueled by large external flows from developed markets and credit (often fueled by crony capitalism) by domestic banks to fund the expansion.

The India experience – from GFC to the 2018 mini-credit crisis

The Insolvency and Bankruptcy Code had put a lot of power in the hands of the providers of capital, the banks, to force defaulting promoters out of management and get stronger players in the saddle. Steel majors like Essar Steel, Bhushan Steel, Bhushan Power and Steel, cement majors like Jaiprakash Associates and Binani either lost their companies or were forced to sell large parts of their businesses to stronger companies.

Players like UltraTech, Dalmia Cement and JSW Steel used this time to consolidate their market position in this environment to emerge both stronger and with an ownership of larger capacities. The primary difference was that they played the credit cycle right, invested when asset prices were below replacement cost and at the same time were extremely conscious of leverage in their balance sheet. The same discipline is required from a minority shareholder.

One needs to look at these businesses as long-term

commitments at least at the time of investing. The good news is that as a listed space small investor there is greater ability to change your position when either the facts change or the environment changes. The biggest boon of doing listed space investing is all-time liquidity. There will always be a willing buyer for an asset at some price. Like Warren Buffett said in his 1987 Berkshire Hathaway shareholder letter: 'Without fail, Mr. Market appears daily and names a price at which he will either buy your interest or sell you his.' This luxury is often not available to promoters and larger institutional shareholders, who may find that there are no buyers for larger blocks at a given price, creating a larger gulf between the buy-ask spread.

This has led to consolidation of assets and pricing power, which is creating large producer surpluses, also allowing them to deleverage in the process. The government has managed to keep its budgetary deficit financing in control, keeping a tab on inflation, and generally interest rates have been stable or trending down.

The cement sector's EBITDA/tonne has increased from a low of INR 792 in Q3 FY 18 to INR 1,254 in Q1 of FY 20 *(source: HDFC Securities Research report)*, and this is on the back of better clinker utilization rates and capacity utilization for most players. While the capacity utilization for the industry was around 65% from FY 14 to FY 18, the capacity utilization in FY 19 and FY 20 is trending north of 70%.

One must also be willing to average up, as the earnings move and the prices also move. Other factors to keep in mind are government policies and the inflation rate. Some governments are lenient with larger deficits in their annual budgets and some are not. Also inflation often forces a government's hand to start increasing interest rates. Either of these in themselves are not sell signals, but if interest rates again look to have a secularly upward trend, it may be worthwhile to have a relook at the thesis. India in the late 2010s had a prolonged period of over-absorption in consumption goods coupled with very little new capex.

Unfortunately, in spite of all these parameters improving for most industries and economies, India had its own mini credit cycle burst in 2018 when IL&FS went bankrupt and the government had to intervene to save it. The NBFC (non-banking financial company) industry in India till then had been consistently heading north, with falling cost of borrowings and better NIMs (net interest margin) on their lending.

According to a PwC-ASSOCHAM report, the market share of NBFCs in the total credit book increased from 12% in FY 08 to 18% in FY 18 and those of private sector banks increased from 18% to 24%. The cost of borrowing for NBFCs, which was at 10.2% in 2013-14, decreased to 8.2% in FY 18. This created a huge delta in the earnings of NBFCs, encouraging them to raise more capital and chase market share.

The quality of lending started to get compromised at the altar of market share, like it always happens in an upward credit cycle. However, as cheap capital started to evaporate, the asset quality also started to get questioned, creating a negative spiral that would eventually eat up many NBFCs, including some large ones.

The mini credit cycle bust had a serious impact on some of the sectors that were dependent on credit for their end-user demand. Real estate and the automobile-component industry were impacted the worst. While real estate had been in the doldrums for quite some time, and the bankruptcies and delays in offering possession by builders had led to a sustained crisis in confidence on the consumer side, real estate has also started to see sustained periods of apathy from providers of capital of all forms. The problem has been even more acute in residential and under-construction segments of the real estate industry.

The problem on the auto-component side started with challenges with respect to NBFCs not being able to lend to customers due to stress in their own balance sheets, and also from increase in interest rates. The problem somewhat got accentuated in metros with increasing penetration of shared mobility through Uber and Ola.

With most stable and large economies there is a pot of gold on either sides of a credit upcycle and a disaster in between. The earlier slopes are the times to increase capital, and the higher peaks are when you start de-allocating.

With a sustained pain in the real estate industry over the last decade, new launches have been suffering. In fact, according to an ANAROCK report, all the way from 2016 to 2019 India saw sales outstrip new launches and a continuous decline in unsold inventory. While the inflation index and wages have been increasing, capital costs have been somewhat stable for almost a decade now, and one does feel that there is pent-up demand in the industry.

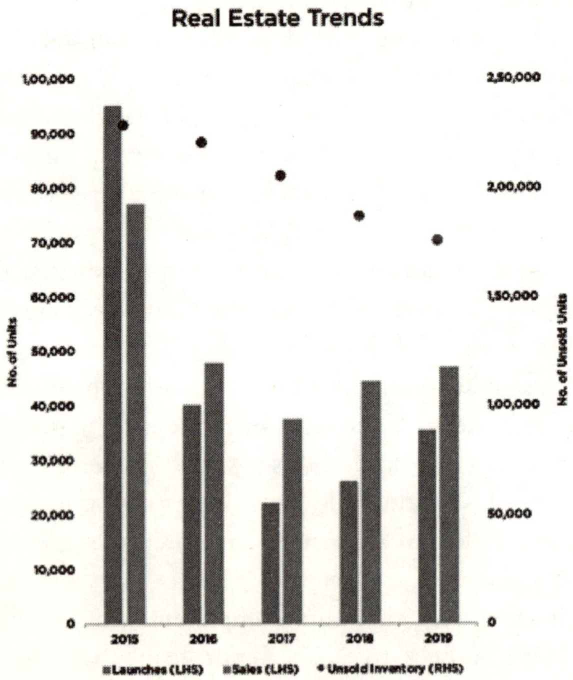

Source: Anarock Capital

As an investor who likes to play cycles, one would like to think that real estate and auto industry stocks, which are deeply battered, could be multi-baggers in the next bull run. There is no harm in getting into a cyclical conviction stock slightly early on; if one waits too long, one may miss the initial run-up. However, one needs to be careful about the risks associated with these propositions.

Similarly, the auto industry, which has suffered quite a bit due to this mini credit crisis and shared mobility, may suffer a bit more due to Covid-19, but eventually the pent-up demand will catch up. Very high quality auto-component companies are available at mouth-watering prices due to the Covid crisis. The Covid crisis may even push the government to continuously keep interest rates low and build a case against shared mobility.

Strategies for investing in a credit cycle

A credit upcycle invariably comes with a stock market bubble. Like in all market bubbles, but specifically in credit cycle bubbles, investors need to be extremely wary of both their capital allocation and leverage. Asset classes at the forefront in terms of attractiveness for providers of capital need to be avoided. If they are leveraged even more so, this is also the time to take some money off the table and gradually move to being at least 40-50% in cash or cash equivalents.

Another very important aspect is where one parks debt. Avoid NBFCs, smaller banks and corporate deposits like the plague. Credit risk mutual funds and public NCDs (non-convertible debenture) should also be avoided, even if it means sacrificing multiple percentage points of yield. In a credit cycle, one needs to be absolutely sure that their cash and cash equivalents are absolutely safe. Strong nationalized banks, large well-capitalized banks, G-Secs and triple A-rated instruments of stable business houses that have no financial services business or a levered distressed business are the ones to go for.

When a businessman has a principal business threatened and levered, there is always an incentive to take money out of their financial services business to invest in their core businesses, even if that money is held in agency and not entirely as owners. The size of the group may often become meaningless, as what may appear too big to fail may also be too large to save. Having money in different pockets is also a good idea. We have already seen multiple examples of such indiscretions with players in India.

As an equity investor, I have never been a great fan of taking credit risks on the money I lend. Why would I want to risk my principal for 3-4% of extra yield? Also, I look at these debt investments as temporary investments that I want to be liquid and available when I want to invest in the markets. For similar reasons, I also do not like debt investments (apart from what I am saving for retirement and for tax benefits) to be invested in instruments that are locked-in for multiple years. A multiple-year lock-in could again mean that capital is not available for when you need it the most or when market presents obvious opportunities.

Higher interest rates make a lot of low-margin commodity businesses unviable, real estate becomes a reverse compounding machine for those having leverage on their books. Bankruptcies offer quality assets to stronger incumbents at less than replacement value, without having to spend time, money and energy of going through project development and build out challenges.

However, this is not a one-sided cycle. There are times when economies go through a protracted period of high-interest rates, under-investment, bankruptcies amongst commodity players and under-investments in greenfield capacities. The rate of investment in new capacities is continuously lower than the secular growth rate of consumption.

New public sector capex is also impacted, and only the strong well-entrenched players with good cash flows look capable and eager to expand capacities. Good quality assets are sometimes available at less than half of their replacement values.

This is the time when governments and central banks are compelled to progressively reduce interest rates to nudge entrepreneurs to undertake more capex. Government spending also increases to fill the void being created by the private sector. Wiser governments would undertake most of these capex in the infrastructure domain, as it creates employment and at the same time has an overall multiplier effect on the economy.

This is the time to get back into sectors that will benefit disproportionately from falling interest rates. The obvious answer may be those with high leverage on their balance sheet. Well, this is where one can make higher returns if you are right, and right quickly, but this is also a riskier strategy. In the early phase of identifying such assets, one must avoid leverage and leveraged companies. The cycles often take longer than expected to play out and leveraged companies' value and worth keep getting impacted by reverse compounding in the interim.

Trailing twelve months (TTM) P/Es have little meaning as earnings are seriously depressed and a Polycycle Investor needs to look at the average of multi-year earnings, may be even 5-10 year earnings. In the case of real estate, one needs to look at the portfolio of the company, and whether they are playing in the right product segment and right geographies.

However, one needs to be wary of product life cycle, and would think an auto component space player in a segment not impacted by electrification of vehicles is the safest bet. Tyre companies, makers of body parts and plastic parts in cars, may all stand to benefit. Also, larger auto-component players with diversified and scaling capabilities may become a go-to player for leaders in the auto electrification phase as new auto OEMs (original equipment manufacturer) would prefer to partner with them to build out the ecosystem. The product life-cycle risk may be a tad too high to bet on large automotive OEMs from a longer-term horizon. Auto-component space gives a natural diversification advantage, and may also benefit from shifting of manufacturing base from some of the countries like China.

Rebalancing portfolio

While we will cover risk mitigation in greater detail in the book, as a multi-decade wealth-creating investor, it is imperative to understand that never mix your own leverage with leverage in the stock you invest in. It's a recipe for disaster. You may make money a couple of times, but somewhere along the way the disaster will be so big that it will cause permanent damage to your portfolio, which in all likelihood will far exceed the money you made earlier.

Also, what is important in credit cycles is to not only reduce allocation to stocks but for one to re-balance one's portfolio. As the cycle moves up, one needs to progressively keep getting out of aggressive sectors in the center of the bull run to get into defensives. The ones which are free of leverage, the ones whose demand is not dependent beyond a point on access to capital.

An easy way to identify these companies is companies that have a consistent dividend payout track record. A consistent and decent payout track record is in many ways a proxy for businesses that will not need to keep re-investing disproportionate amounts of money to maintain their growth and to capture market share.

Also, companies that are unlevered and in the consumption space for non-luxury goods also typically fall into this category. Their consumption does not wither away as quickly as consumption of some of industrial goods, commodities and even luxury goods. While reallocating during the credit cycle or allocating after a credit cycle, market often gives you an opportunity to buy market leaders in niche industries at a relatively cheaper valuation.

One would do well to identify industries that are between half a billion dollars in size to two billion dollars' size and growing at a rapid rate. These industries often fall outside the radar of institutional investors and research houses. At the same time, they are unlikely to be disrupted by a large investment by Mr. Moneybags who wants to capture market share.

Industry leaders in these spaces are often financially strong and enjoy a decent brand and market position to get pricing premium. For example, Hawkins Cookers Ltd., one of India's top two companies making pressure cookers, was available at 6x PE in 2008 and more than 5% dividend yield. The per share price was hovering around INR 150-170 per share well into 2009. The stock has created tremendous shareholder value and from being a INR 75 crores market cap company in 2008 went up to being a INR 2,500 crores market cap company in 2020. All through this period, paying handsome dividend back to its shareholders. One such stock, with a decent capital allocation to it, can have a life-changing impact on one's portfolio and wealth creation.

On the other hand, another company that grew multi-fold all the way till 2008 is Jaiprakash Associates. A large EPC (engineering, procurement and construction) company, it leveraged and raised debt like nobody's business to expand capacity in cement, power and real estate. A stock market darling for its execution capabilities, it demonstrated an ability to scale up large cement plants, very complex and large hydropower projects and townships.

With extremely high leverage and exposure to businesses that were seeing margins and profitability dip and an evaporation of demand in real estate, Jaiprakash Associates was in the middle of a perfect storm. The company had to sell its best cement assets to UltraTech to pay off debts. Its power subsidiary, Jaiprakash Power Ventures, was taken over by the lenders, and its expressway and real estate subsidiary, Jaypee Infratech, went into insolvency and was handed over to state-run Navratna PSU NBCC. The stock price of Jaiprakash Associates, which was once trading at more than INR 300 a piece, now with multiple dilutions at multiple levels, trades at barely INR 1.5 per share in 2020, completely crippled by debt at multiple levels and falling operating performances of each of their businesses.

There will be multiple arguments made for the demise of such groups, including corporate governance, adverse market environment etc. But experience suggests there is no bigger sin or enemy than holding on to unsustainable debt in an adverse climate. If one has the balance sheet, the noise around some of the other issues can make a dent, but one does survive to tell the tale.

Behavioural biases

Equity investing in the best of times is a risky proposition. There are multiple ways one can look at investing. I have seen investors betting consistently on quality stocks with a long-term track record of secular growth and beating benchmark returns on a long-term basis. It is relatively easier and the obvious thing to do for a lot of investors; there is merit in allocating a pool of your equity portfolio to such investments.

However, these investors are also not immune to cyclical pains. ICICI Bank, which was the darling of investors till 2008 and a flag-bearer of emerging private sector banks in the country, virtually gave no returns for10 years from January 2008 to July 2018.

Motherson Sumi Systems, which was again the blue-eyed boy in the Indian auto-component sector and created tremendous wealth for shareholders up until 2018, was trading at virtually a third of its peak two years down the line due to the crisis in the auto-component space.

Even good stocks become not so good if you pay up disproportionately for them. Both these stocks were hit by credit cycle – ICICI Bank got hit by GFC in 2008 and Motherson Sumi Systems by the mini-credit crisis in the NBFC space in India. A credit cycle-conscious investor will probably be a little bit more aware of how cycles can impact their profitability and multiples. No one can exit at peak or enter at an absolute bottom consistently, but being conscious of different cycles does improve your portfolio performance dramatically. One may not have had been able to identify challenges in Motherson Sumi Systems till the crisis actually happened, but one could have made an exit before a large decline in its share price.

Also, many of these trailblazers often trade at a significant premium to their peers. The market often assumes that these companies will continue their growth momentum for the foreseeable future and will further consolidate their market leadership position. Often it is more difficult to do that over multiple decades and something somewhere gives way. When something like this happens, not only the earnings contract, multiples contract even more rapidly, which leads to a double whammy for investors in these stocks.

Burnt by leveraging during the GFC, many fancy forms of investing like 'moat investing', 'paying up for quality' and 'coffee can investing' have come to the fore. While some of the tools mentioned by these theorists are fantastic, the false sense of security it preaches can be catastrophic. Most of the examples taken to elucidate the success of these styles of investing suffer hugely from survivorship and hindsight bias[2].

Now let's look at some high-quality consumer stocks that one would have assumed to be extremely high quality with decades of

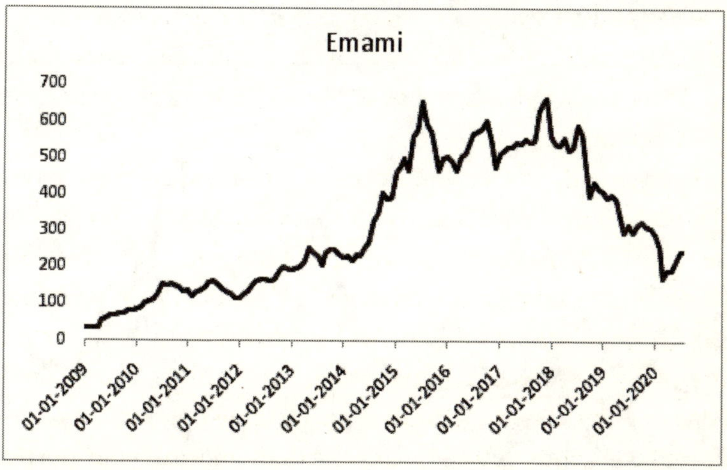

Emami share price trend

2. Survivorship bias indicates extrapolating the success of survivors to believe that it represents the entire population. Hindsight bias is the tendency of people to overestimate their ability to predict things after the event has happened, which otherwise they could not have predicted.

track record of performance. Emami, which was in the FMCG space and created tremendous shareholder value all the way up to 2017, looked very different in 2017. What was the difference between an Emami or a Marico?

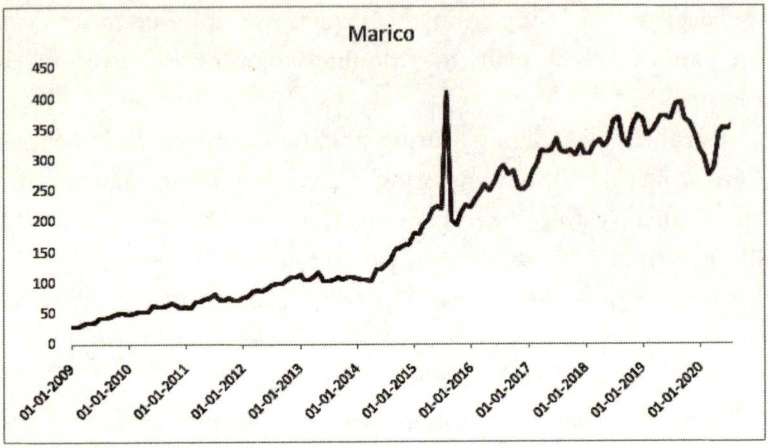

Marico share price trend

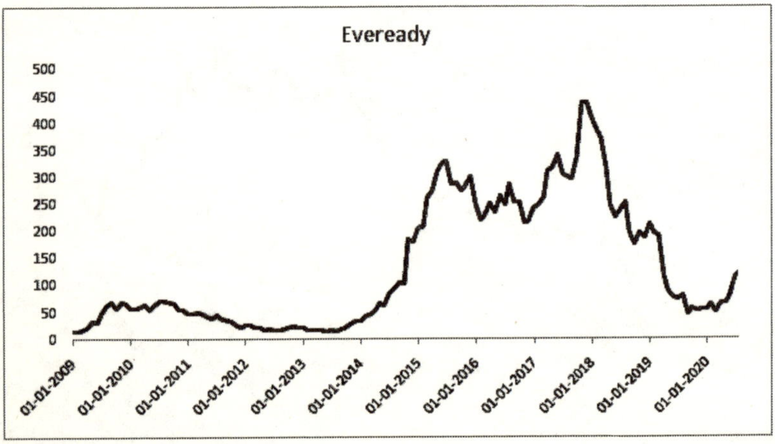

Eveready share price trend

Both Emami and Marico looked fairly alike till 2017 in terms of their stock market performance in quality FMCG space, with an extremely strong track record of value creation. However, a few things went wrong with the Emami group. After a blaze in its co-founded AMRI hospital, it diversified into capital-hungry businesses like cement, putting its balance sheet under stress, and pledged shares from the FMCG business to raise debt for other businesses. Same is true with Eveready. Probably both Eveready and Emami would have found their way, with most investors wanting to invest in quality. They did create lot of value till the 2018 mini-credit crisis started impacting their businesses.

Not that there is no virtue in picking quality stocks and holding them for a long time. In fact, quite the contrary; I do believe there are such stocks and they should find a place in every equity investor's portfolio. What the investor needs to do is to know his position at all points of time and figure out what are the red flags to avoid, impact of cycles, allocation of capital within the group, promoter level leverage etc. Perfectly good businesses can be killed by poor capital allocation decisions.

No matter what is one's investing style, there is huge merit in being conscious of the cycles that affect the stock you own. And credit cycle is a super-cycle hiding multiple cycles within it; it has an impact on not only financial services business, but many other businesses and sometimes, like in the case of GFC, across major economies of the world. Missing the cycles can make one feel like the musicians on the Titanic, who played on helplessly to soothe nerves while the ship kept sinking.

3

Market Cycle

The market cycle is one cycle that has been extensively covered in a lot of literature on stock-market investing. Books have been written on greed and fear, movies have been made; gloom, boom and doom are phrases that have become a part of market vocabulary.

Most market cycles have a leader of the pack, a certain sector or a certain theme leads the rally, and when the darlings of the market start to get ahead of themselves, investors continuously keep widening their horizons to add more sectors and companies to their bucket, creating a wider market rally. The trend reverses when the markets become overheated, and the sector leaders which drove the rally are the first ones to experience the pain, and other sectors follow. The fall on some occasions is so steep that deep pockets of values again start getting created.

The cycles vary in intensity and duration, but they are as certain as death. Markets do and will follow the law of averages, and will eventually revert to their long-term mean. Most investors, stock market or otherwise, invest with a rear-view mirror. They all want to participate in asset classes that have created value for investors in the last couple of months or years, mostly ignorant that eventually markets will revert to their mean. Some individual stocks may continue to outperform the market based on their underlying performance, but eventually they will also revert to their mean multiples.

The primary emotions that drive market cycles are the feeling of being left out, envy, greed and fear. If emotions are what drive markets, it is fairly difficult to always assume the efficient market hypothesis. Algorithm trading is trying to take out bits of emotions from trading, but I still feel most algorithms fail to have a full understanding of cycles, businesses, or have been made by coders who fail to look at investing as a multi-decade activity. Increasingly, algorithm trading will reduce pockets of deep undervaluation by identifying extremely cheap stocks – this is where a value investor has to find new tools and new mechanisms to find pockets of deep value. Obvious pockets of undervaluation using old-hat screeners like price to earnings multiples, dividend yield etc. will become more and more difficult to come by.

To that extent, I feel that investors and practitioners of value investing and long-term investing will continue to find themes and mental models to outsmart the algorithms for a fairly long time. Not sure whether traders will continue to have that advantage even in medium term. Not being my area of competence, I will refrain from commenting unduly on sustainability of business models for day trading and technical analysis.

Strategies to play market gyrations

These market cycles present and will continue to present tremendous money-making opportunities for investors. Unlike some of the other cyclical plays, play on market cycles can give opportunities to even a passive, unsophisticated investor with some tools to help in beating index performance over a longer term. The other kinds of cycle plays require a greater degree of involvement, sophistication and understanding of the economy than this one.

I think the easiest tool is to buy more when markets are cheap and buy less when they are expensive. This is one philosophy that has created hordes of SIP (systemic investment plan) investors for mutual funds. SIP is a way of investment where investors allocate equal amounts of money at regular periodic intervals, mostly monthly. This helps in dollar cost averaging, automatically ensuring that you are buying more units when the NAV is lower and lesser number of units when the market is higher. With this simple tool a disciplined investor can beat market returns over a long term by just investing in index funds through the SIP route.

SIP in index funds is probably one of the easiest and sure-shot way of beating index returns over a longer term without having to apply one's mind to investing decisions, and I recommend that everyone who does not have the ability or time to invest money directly in stocks must have a SIP. However, there are ways to increase the margin between benchmark returns and portfolio returns even more.

Typically, most stock markets have a Goldilocks zone within which they trade and there is also a trend towards where this Goldilocks zone is moving. I feel India currently trades in the zone of 15x PE in bear markets and 24x to 30x in a bull market with a minor upward bias towards where this range is moving. Even a mutual fund investor can benefit from this understanding and power his SIP linked to multiples. One can make mental models to activate that. For instance, if market PE is less than 16, I put twice the amount in SIP; if it is between 16 and 20, one can put 1.5x of the usual SIP amount and halve the SIP contribution when the multiples start going north of 25.

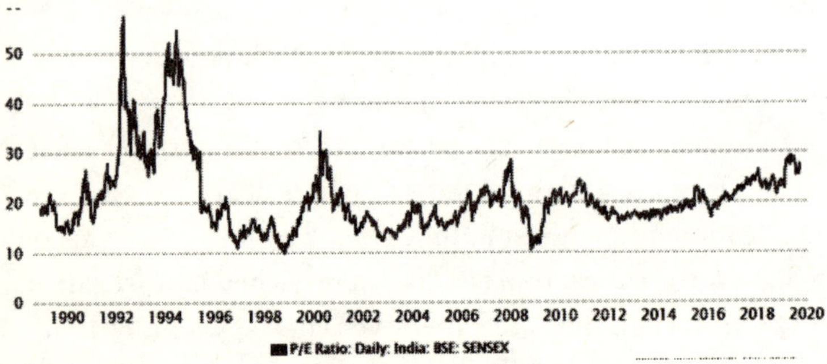

Source: WWW.CEICDATA.COM | CEIC Data

A direct stock investor can take even more pronounced bets and, in fact, de-allocate capital when the multiples start becoming uncomfortable. The moment I see the index PE inching towards 24x, I am keen to start looking at my portfolio to see what can I sell, and keep on taking money off the market, especially from sectors that have become very frothy. Similarly, as soon as indices start to go south of 20x, I start itching to find the next market darling, sectors that can do well in the incumbent environment, where there could be an upcycle coming. Although, for most of the times it is not advisable to leverage to invest in stocks, if indices go south of 15x and I get quality stocks above a dividend yield of 4-5%, it may not be a bad idea to leverage and invest in those stocks.

Are there exceptions to the above rule? Sure, there are. The two exceptions that readily come to mind are rapid currency devaluation and war. If the government of the day gets too aggressive to print its way out of fiscal deficit, the currency can lose the trust of all players and permanently damage not only businesses but the overall working of the economy, leading to a permanent flight of capital and civil unrests. We will cover some of those examples later. The other exception is a full-scale war. A war can damage assets, earnings, manpower, the fiscal health of an economy for over a decade.

Apart from these two exceptions, there are not too many cases that impair the earning ability of an economy permanently or for a very long time. With markets in low teens and quality stocks available at a high dividend yield, there is precious little that can go wrong over a longer period of time. There may be times that a left-leaning government may impair businesses and may come up with policies that are not conducive for businesses, but eventually those policies have their own way of coming back to bite, causing political change and new governments. Democracy has its own checks and balances. Though overturning democracy and becoming a dictatorship like our neighbouring country is another matter completely.

Greater competence, greater delta

Apart from these simpler passive and semi-passive strategies, there are options in front of a slightly more sophisticated investor to make an even greater delta on long-term portfolio returns by a more active portfolio management strategy. This requires a greater study of the stocks one owns or wants to own. I normally advise investors to have a basic understanding and competencies across at least five sectors and understanding of businesses and fair valuation of 35-40 stocks. This creates a circle of competence and allows investors to have an ongoing sense of fair value of those businesses.

The fair valuation is not necessarily a static number but changes with performance, management quality, decisions they make and the environment. A range with a 10-15% variation either sides of the mid-point is something one can safely work with.

Once we have a sense of fair value of a stock on a stable market basis, it becomes that much easier to set entry and exit points for the stock. How much to put in and how much to sell are often determined by the liquidity position of the investor.

In a bear market, the investor should clearly identify the areas from where he can generate additional liquidity, whether it is loan against shares, loan against property or other investments, withdrawal or loan against long-term savings accounts like employee provident fund etc. Although, exercising these leverage calls should be done only in exceptional circumstances (say, when market PE falls below 15), one should not be left twiddling thumbs when markets present the opportunities of a lifetime.

Having liquidity and ability to invest at the right time can create enormous shareholder wealth. It is the mother of dollar cost averaging. It is a blessing to be able to double down on your high conviction stocks at more than 50-60% discount to their fair value. Suppose a stock with a fair market value of INR 100 is trading at INR 40 per share due to adverse market conditions, in five years the stock goes to INR 200 per share. The returns for an investor who is able to buy the stock at INR 40 per share becomes five times instead of two that he would have made if he had bought at fair value.

Agency challenges for fund managers

While charters of mutual fund provide great security from improper capital allocation and mala fides of agency business, and the restrictions stipulated in those charters should be there, they also tie the hands of fund managers in terms of taking capital allocation calls. However, a mutual fund investor can still play on cycles, by reducing exposure to their equity-linked mutual funds as markets go up and selling when markets go down. Often it is difficult to take out money from an investment which in near term is giving better returns than any other asset class, but it does add tremendous impetus to long-term portfolio returns. It also helps one create liquidity to invest a larger pool in the same mutual funds when markets are at a significantly lower level. Rear-view mirror investing is one of the biggest dampeners to long-term portfolio returns. Investors who keep putting in more and more money into asset classes that have given superior near-term return often remind me of one of the warnings found in rear-view mirrors in a lot of vehicles: 'The objects in the mirror are closer than they appear.'

There are a couple of other agency problems that mutual fund managers face. The first one is what we call 'cover your ass' syndrome, where fund managers are encouraged to allocate more and more capital to large-cap safer stocks and are relatively unwilling to take bets on more lucrative mid-cap and small-cap companies. If a bet goes wrong on a large-cap company, one is unlikely to be hauled up, but if a mid-cap call goes seriously wrong, one is held answerable for the call.

Another agency problem is that as a fund manager your growth and remuneration is typically linked to the AUM (asset under management) you run. There is very little incentive for a fund manager to say no to money that is on the table even if he feels that there are very few lucrative investment opportunities for the fund manager to work with.

In the period from 2016 to early 2020, this problem got seriously accentuated. With a prolonged slump in real estate, demonetization, flat gold prices and vigilance on black money in the system, a secular uptick in stock markets, and effective campaigning by mutual funds, the Indian middle class got enamoured of the SIP phenomena. It kept giving returns for an extended period, creating a positive feedback loop and encouraging greater allocation to SIPs, and new investors kept joining the bandwagon.

The Indian mutual fund managers were saddled with more money than worthwhile opportunities, and they kept investing in top quality, less risky sectors like FMCG, consumer and large financial services and banks, creating a bubble in quality stocks. The multiples for some leading FMCG stocks and consumer companies were at over 50x P/E and those of quality financial services at 4-6x book value. I guess every cycle has its own frontrunners for a bubble.

The curse of frontrunners

Early 2000 saw a tech bubble where technology company prices went through the roof. Companies with no background in technology started adding info, tech, technologies and soft to their name. The euphoria was such that just the name change would make the stock run up. Tech darlings like Patni, Satyam Computers, Pentasoft and many other tech companies that were market darlings at the time of the tech boom have all been relegated to the dustbins of history. Even high quality companies and eventual leaders like Infosys and Wipro gave sustained periods of no-returns when gotten into in the middle of the tech bull run.

Similarly, the 2004-2007 rally, which coincided with the global credit super-cycle, created many cycles. The frontrunners, in my view, for this cycle were real estate, infrastructure and basic goods like cement, steel etc. Because credit was cheap and liquidity was ample, the sectors that could deploy large pools of capex to grow invited more interest from the providers of capital. Every banker and investor on the street was more worried about the deal size than deal quality. I still remember that as a banker we used to joke that on smaller deals you don't get your ROTI (return on time invested).

I think the best way to identify favourite sectors in a particular cycle is to look at which sector has maximum IPOs (initial public offering) or large fundraises. Clearly, business owners know when they are getting maximum bang for their buck, and barring distress situations they would want to raise equity money when it is available and available cheap.

The entire real estate and infrastructure sector was damaged beyond recognition post-2008 crisis. Corruption scandals in allocation of mining resources, government contracts, land banks and the telecom spectrum created an environment of both pessimism and despondency among investors in these sectors. Investors lost a lot of money, and with de-allocation of resources in some of their portfolio companies, there was little hope of revival in those investments.

The power sector, which was another darling of the street with high merchant power tariffs (purchasing electricity at market rates on short-term contracts or on spot prices vis-à-vis the traditional practice of long-term contracts usually signed on a cost-plus basis) and deficits between demand and consumption, was also attracting entrepreneurs and investors. Most power plants looking to raise money had coal linkages from the ministry of power, which till that time investors believed to be a comfort letter from the government of India. Then Coal India went on road for its own IPO and suddenly the investor community realised that the coal linkage given by the ministry of power was far from sacrosanct. To compound the problem, Indonesia had a change in coal pricing and the Indian government de-allocated a number of coalmines under a Supreme Court order. Further, the health of state electricity boards (SEBs) was so damaged that the tariff recoveries with some of them started getting impacted. To sum it up, everything that could have gone wrong did go wrong.

After an interim spike in 2010 and 2011, the markets continued to trade below 20x PE from end-2011 to mid-2013, which formed the base for the next cyclical upturn. The advent of a new government came with new hope for the markets, which started to head towards the next upcycle. Some of the policy measures to bring transparency in allocation of resources, procurement and real estate meant that the capital chasing these assets came down, as the return delta was lower.

Between 2016 and 2018, demonetization and GST (goods and services tax) were implemented, which led to a faster formalisation of the economy and 'financialisation' of savings. In other words, the savings of the middle class started moving from assets like real estate and gold to financial instruments like equities, mutual fund, debt papers etc. This created a mini-credit cycle and a plethora of new NBFCs and lending models between 2016 and 2018. While the real interest rates continued to be high, nominal interest rates were softening, which pushed investors and providers of capital to reach out for higher yielding, and by definition higher risk debt assets. Also, public sector banks burnt by NPAs were ceding market share to NBFCs and were happy to lend to NBFCs as against lending to corporates directly. The underlying assumption was that probably these private-sector NBFCs have a better credit evaluation and pricing capability than some of the public sector banks. The assumption initially had some merit also but increasingly buoyed by the available liquidity, the NBFCs started to take riskier bets.

This made investors wary of NBFCs as an investment class. They continued to be averse to real estate, infrastructure and gold, creating further concentration of investments in large FMCG and large banks. The multiples of 50x-70x for FMCG companies became the new normal. It is difficult to imagine that some of these assets will continue to create superior returns for investors over a long period at these multiples. Also, what investors need to be wary of is the reinvestment risk. Can these FMCG giants continue to reinvest their profits to generate similar returns?

Technology has somewhat democratized the marketplace, allowing smaller entrepreneurs a reach through e-commerce and modern trade, which was earlier never available to them. The ability to market your produce on internet, where one can pay per click instead of having to pay astronomical sums for space in mainstream media and television, clearly created a chasm too big to bridge. Increasingly, smaller players are finding ways to nibble on some market share in niche products where the big boys are not very well entrenched.

This market cycle has also brought another bubble of e-commerce, social media platforms, aggregators and multiple other SaaS (software as a service) and internet-based business models like Uber, Ola, Paytm, Oyo, Lenskart, Zerodha, MakeMyTrip and PolicyBazaar to name a few. Many of these models are dependent on large funding to continue to grow their business, and burning cash for customer acquisition and market access. Business models that can find ways to become profitable on a sustainable basis and add value in this era of disruption will create sustainable value. While a lot of these companies remain unlisted and have been raising private capital, they will need to find sustainable path to profitability at some point.

It is counter-intuitive to be talking about off-market investments in the section on market cycle, but this has become too large to ignore and the impact it now has on some of the businesses in the listed space is hard to ignore. An understanding of these models is becoming an imperative to grasp market cycles and product life cycles a little more. We will continue to talk about these businesses to have a more nuanced understanding of businesses worth owning in this environment.

These businesses are a huge force of market disruption and disintermediation. Product distribution margins, services distribution margins like for insurance and mutual funds, shared mobility, travel – they are all disrupting large healthy businesses like never before. I have no doubt that fee-based earnings for large banks and financial services firms will continue to be under pressure over the next decade. At 1-2% commission, financial services distribution was a low-margin business and difficult to replicate in a brick and mortar world. Only banks and other large players with their distribution capabilities could have competed, but suddenly in a world of digital access, it has stopped being a significant barrier to entry.

Even though NBFCs will go through their own pain cycle, tech-based and AI (artificial intelligence) based lending models will nibble on the market share of large lenders. Some of these trends are going to get more pronounced as technology and access to technology become increasingly cheaper and ubiquitous. However, for the larger banks, a cheaper source of capital through current account and savings account will continue to be a differentiator difficult to compete with.

Calling leaders of the next bull run

Sitting in early 2020, how to identify sectors to invest in for the next bull run? A broad rule is that sectors that missed the boat in the previous bull run and have been out of favour with investors for a very long time will make a comeback. However, some sectors that are in a declining product life cycle curve may never come back.

So one should look at industries that are seriously underinvested in and are, hence, creating a favourable supply side story. We discussed real estate and auto-components in earlier chapters; packaging materials have been out of favour for almost a decade, but it is difficult to write them off. After the mega bull run the sector had in 2010, which caused large capacity additions, the additions to the industry has been somewhat trailing or barely keeping pace with increasing demand. One would think that signs of revival for the real estate industry will get pronounced as the 2020s roll on.

Large steel players may see fortunes turning, with consolidation in the industry and very limited new capacity addition in the recent past. Averseness of providers of capital to take bets in these industries has further accentuated the problem. Not only equity, even lenders are reluctant to take exposure to large greenfield steel plants.

Building materials, agro-chemicals, specialty chemicals may create scale and give superior returns. By and large, one would be inclined to believe that in the next decade, in terms of portfolio returns, manufacturing is likely to give superior returns vis-à-vis consumer and services. A Polycycle Investor will do well to have some of the interesting themes around manufacturing on their radar.

It's always riskier to do crystal ball gazing when you do not have the benefit of hindsight, but that is where investing temperament is tested. Having a contrarian investing temperament and to look at sectors others are not looking at is the road to riches in investing.

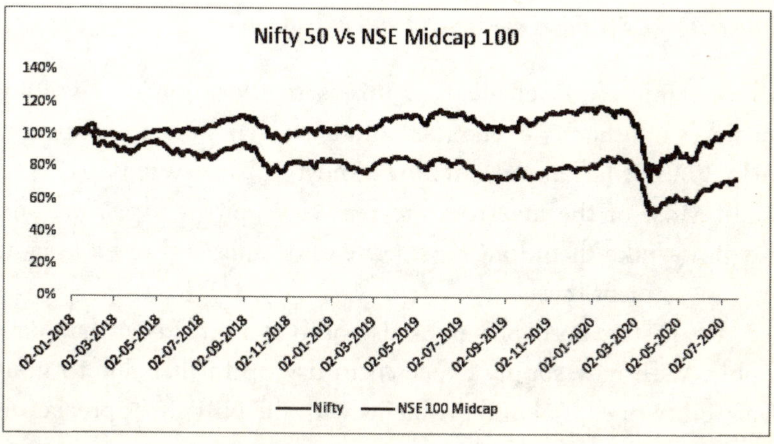

The other area of under-investment in this cycle has been the mid-cap space. In the last two years while the Nifty 50 was up by 7%, the mid-cap space corrected by 26%. The SIP mobilisation increased from INR 3,127 crores in the beginning of FY 17 to over INR 8,327 crores by the beginning of FY 21. Clearly, there is a surfeit of new investments in equity-linked mutual funds. However, one has to understand that a lot of these new investors, who have joined the SIP bandwagon in those three years, would have now seen negative returns. If the Covid-related downturn continues, it is hard to imagine that the SIP flows will not be disrupted.

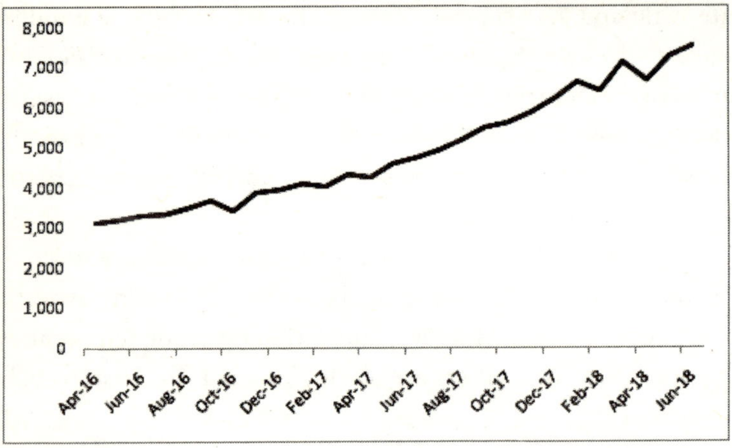

Source: AMFI, SIP flows in Mutual Fund in INR Crores

Another interesting element of this is re-allocation of investing surpluses in other asset classes. Gold has given fantastic returns in early 2020. It has appreciated by almost 70% between 2017 and 2020. Most of the investors are rear-view mirror investors, and it will not take them long to start re-allocating and re-looking at their investment thesis.

Real estate absorption has also been at a rate faster than new supply. With new supply expected to dry up further due to non-availability of capital and problems with the NBFCs, appreciation in residential real estate will follow. Once that happens, there will be further re-allocation of capital to real estate as an asset class.

Like stock markets have their cycles, other asset classes have their own cycles. Each of these asset classes keep getting into and out of favour with investors from time to time. A student of investing will do well to understand these trends and have the tools to understand how human beings behave in times like these. Rear-view investors often miss what is coming up in front of them, and tend to extrapolate near-term performance over longer durations.

Another very interesting aspect of an upcycle is increasing wages, which improves surpluses with the middle class and especially with the investing class. The ability to sell previously held positions at higher values gives an investor both liquidity and confidence to take new positions. It also often instills confidence in one's own ability in stock picking, which may or may not always be correct.

Timing allocation of capital

A market upcycle is accompanied by greater capital market activity like IPOs, bigger fund raises by private equity investors, and often softening interest rate, artificially bringing down risk perception for all providers of capital. To many it may sound counter-intuitive, but often the best time to park money in high-quality debt and cash equivalents is when yields are low and stock markets are at all-time highs, and PE multiples start moving into the red zone north of 25x.

It might sound easy to do, but it is very difficult to leave a party where everyone looks glamorous, music is playing and food is great. This is where temperament and a deep-seated understanding of market cycles help investors to leave for home and not feel bad about losing out on the fun. There is always a brawl here or a puke there waiting at the end of every great party.

Also, what is extremely important for a market cycle player is to identify the difference between corrections within a bull run and a cyclical downturn. As a thumb-rule, typically when the market re-traces more than 20% from its highs, that is when one would think that markets are going in for a cyclical downturn. There are other indicators or a black swan event like the tech bubble bursting; GFC led to bankruptcy at Lehman Brothers and Bear Stearns. Multiple large intra-day corrections, when followed by a major systemic risk event typically, indicate that the bear market may persist for some time.

In the initial period of the crash, the market keeps finding new money coming in at every new level, because both investors and analysts have their mental anchoring to 52-week highs. For every significant correction in the market there will be bear market rallies, which will suck in new sets of investors.

It is extremely important to be patient and not get into the 'left-out' trap too early and put large pools of liquidity in the initial phase. One needs to only nibble in the earlier phase, may be even sell positions in those stocks one may not be comfortable holding through the bear market and re-balance one's portfolio. Leaders of the previous bull run need to be let go at a faster pace, and in the initial phase one should invest only in classical value stocks.

What is also important is that a Polycycle Investor needs to be discerning and patient; he needs to keep investing when the markets are trending down, when the markets are in a flat phase at a much lower level and also when the cycle starts turning. Typically, this phase lasts for a period of two to three years. In some cases it could be longer.

The ability to keep increasing allocation to stocks as the markets progressively head south is a great force multiplier. One should typically have at least an 18-month deployment plan for the surplus liquidity, and all pockets of liquidity should be explored and identified. One does feel that Covid-19 is one such event and the investor community will do well not to feel nervous and suffer a left-out syndrome in every correction. Two things that help in breaking this psychosis is to keep nibbling at smaller quantities, say 5% of the investible surplus every month for the first six to eight months, before increasing allocation. Also, watching daily stock market prices and market commentary on television is a sure-shot way to dissolve the resolve.

Indian capital market history

Market cycles are the most obvious and visible forms of a cycle, with enough long-term data available of values of different market indices for a long time. It is also the most tracked and media covered cycle. Still, even sophisticated investors often fail to read them correctly. Only part of it is attributable to the agency problem, and a much larger part attributable to investing looking in the rear-view mirror. Also, trained investors often lack the temperament to look at investing as a multi-decade activity, and the decision-making process and the tools deployed are geared to take care of the next quarter at worst and a three-year time horizon at best. The drag on portfolio returns in intervening quarters while waiting for a cycle to eventually turn is not a luxury afforded to most investors.

Indian markets in the 90s were still evolving and not too mature, with limited depth, and prone to manipulation by large stock market operators. In the last two decades, Indian stock markets have created a robust regulatory framework, oversight and technology backbone, making things a lot more transparent and investor-friendly.

One is reminded of the craziest bull run that the Indian markets faced during the early 1990s, which later came to be associated with Harshad Mehta. Morgan Stanley in January 1994 launched a closed-ended growth fund. The fund, which was yet to invest any money in stocks, was trading at almost a 50% grey market premium and there were queues outside the Morgan Stanley office for an initial public offering of a fund. The disappointment of investors saw no bounds when the NAV of the fund fell below par on day one of its listing. To modern-day investors it may sound ridiculous that people were willing to invest in the IPO of a fund at a hefty premium. Twice during the 1992-94 era, the BSE Sensex PE breached 50x, and was above 30x for a period of almost two years. Admittedly, it was immediately in the post-liberalization era, but the economy at best was doing only moderately well and the currency depreciated almost 25% during that period.

The markets were driven by anything but rationality and companies across sectors were trading at stratospheric multiples. Most bull markets have their own craziness and excesses. But the 1992 market cycle was something else. The BSE Sensex, which was around 600-700 in 1990, went over 4,200 in 1994. A 6x return on a mainstream market index in a four-year time frame is the stuff of folklore. Never before, and I sincerely hope never again, have the markets seen such a sustained phase of irrationality in stock market prices. Anyway, a Polycycle Investor has nothing to gain from these super cycles. He will start exiting at a much milder level of 25x and will probably be sitting almost entirely on cash and cash equivalents by the time index multiples hit 35x.

The next market cycle coincided with the tech boom and had its own Pied Piper in Ketan Parekh. There was a group of stocks popularly known as K-10 stocks that predictably were in the space that drove the bull run, which were in information technology, communications and entertainment (popularly known as ICE stocks at that time). Some of the K-10 stocks went 4x to 5x within no time during the bull run. The stock price of Zee Telefilms, for instance, zoomed from INR 127 per share to INR 10,000 per share. *(Source: Wikipedia, www.wolveswealth.com)*. Many others, like Pritish Nandy Communications and Mukta Arts, which hit stratospheric levels in 2000, trade at a tenth of the value two decades hence. Many others. like Crest Communications, Amitabh Bachchan Corporation Ltd. etc, have completely disappeared from the scene. The fact that some market manipulators without any institutional backing could wreak so much havoc on the wider markets to the detriment of smaller investors is scary. Anecdotes like these cement one's belief in relative immaturity and limited regulatory oversight on stock markets in that era.

Both the 1992-94 bull run and the tech boom of the late 1990s were essentially scams where the bubble was fueled by bank money procured by the respective protagonists of the scam by fraudulent means. Bank receipts, stamp papers and forged cheques were used to borrow money to keep funneling them into stocks. Similarly, Ketan Parekh used his network of stock traders and brokers to do circular trading to inflate prices of certain stocks.

This forced multiple changes in the regulatory framework in India, pushing the Reserve Bank of India (RBI) into prohibiting lending for acquisition of shares. Further, institutional frameworks were established for dematerialization of shares which were now held with strong custodians, to put surveillance mechanisms to track circular trading and deter mischief-makers.

The regulator, government, market participants, merchant bankers and the broker community – all of them have contributed immensely to building Indian capital markets to what they are and to creating a strong technology backbone, regulatory framework, disclosures requirements and checks and balances over the years. Today the markets have great institutional depth, global confidence and transparency, where large-scale rigging of stocks is becoming increasingly more difficult and dangerous.

The importance of a well-functioning regulated capital market framework cannot be stressed too much. At one end it gives far greater equity capital access to entrepreneurs and at the other end it gives both institutional and retail investors a relatively level playing field. Almost all global investors worth their name, including sovereign funds, pension funds, long-only hedge funds and fund of funds, want a piece of the Indian growth story. It also has created a greater depth for retail investors, whether they want to participate directly or through mutual funds. The mutual fund industry over the years has regulated itself fantastically well under the umbrella of AMFI (Association of Mutual Funds in India), putting a check on mis-selling, false return assurances and disclosure frameworks. In spite of some of the challenges we discussed about mutual funds, for small investors looking to have a slice of India's growth pie, it probably remains the most efficient vehicle to play the game with.

4

Commodity Cycle

A commodity cycle is one of the most difficult cycles to predict. The best of investors and even well-entrenched players in the same industry often fail to predict them correctly. Probably the most important quality to be able to play this cycle is humility and knowing that you will be wrong multiple times.

These are also sectors that require regular capex to maintain and upgrade one's market position. Regulatory environment and threats from imports often compound the problem and act as variables that are very difficult to predict even in medium term for most of the sophisticated investors. Promoter integrity, bloating project costs to reduce promoter contribution and dependency on mineral and other raw material resources add to business complexities. No wonder the multiples that commodity sector players enjoy are very low and more often than not stocks in the commodity segment are available at single digit P/E multiples.

This is where the attractiveness of a commodity play comes in. One gets high variability in earnings with extremely low multiples. Often multiples expand along with earnings, creating opportunities of a lifetime. When one thinks of commodities, one often starts thinking of only the larger industries in the commodity space like cement, steel, ferro alloys, textile etc. However, the list of commodities is pretty much endless.

Packaging material, rubber, refractories, glass, agricultural produce, agro-chemicals are all commodities, and many other businesses like shipping, building materials like board, sanitary-ware, electricals etc. also often show qualities of being a commodity. While there is a lot of research on mainstream commodities and players in that space, some of the other commodity plays have much smaller players and do not get the desired attention. However, because of nuances involved and a lack of literature, it is often difficult to understand these cycles very well. This is where humility becomes an extremely important quality of a commodity cycle investor; one should always have the diligence of a student while playing the commodity cycles.

Also, it is important to understand that a Polycycle Investor is essentially an investor in common stocks, so if I feel that plastic packaging (BOPP and BoPET) businesses are going to perk up, I will hunt for stocks I like in that space. I will look for companies with a healthy balance sheet, have good promoters and margin of safety in terms of its prevailing market price as against my assessment of its intrinsic value. Holding a stock gives multiple advantages to an investor, vis-à-vis holding the commodity, like greater holding power, lesser holding costs, discovery of mispriced bets and the ability to partner with the player one trusts.

Making commodity plays work

Let us look at some interesting commodity cycles that have had an impact on the overall industry and, in some cases, some of the industries they fed. The packaging industry went through a crazy price uptick in 2010.

A historical depiction of the Industry raw material prices and PET film prices for Far East region is given below.

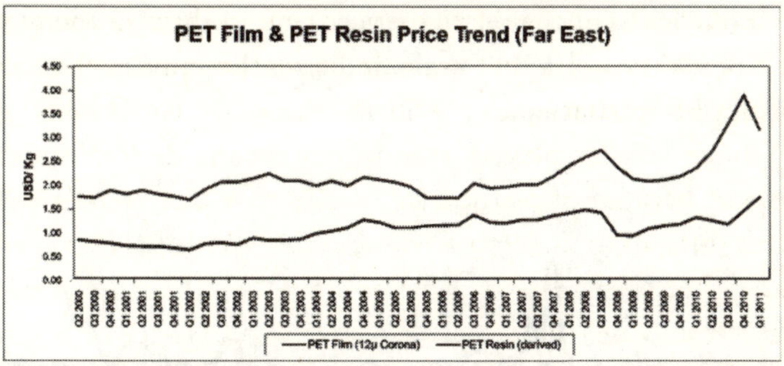

Source: Polyplex annual report

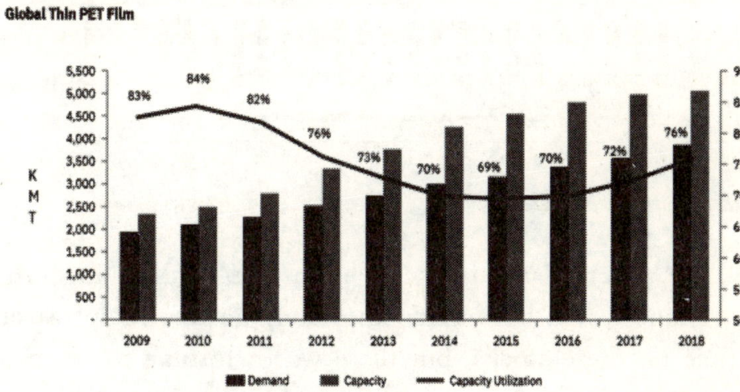

Source: Polyplex annual report

The delta of the resin prices, a key raw material, and the end good prices more than doubled in 2010, creating a wave of capacity addition till 2016. While the demand growth has a secular trend, the capacity additions have a tendency to bunch up. The bunching up of capacities causes demand-supply mismatch and a loss of pricing power with the producers. Leverage of new capex, lower capacity utilisation and lower prices again drive down industry profitability, forcing players to put a stop to their capex cycle. A few years of underinvestment allows demand-supply dynamics to move back in favour of producers, pushing up the capacity utilisation and pricing power back into their hands, again creating an upside potential.

If one looks at the relative price trend of three of the players in the domain of different scale and size, the impact of cycle on stock market performance is evident.

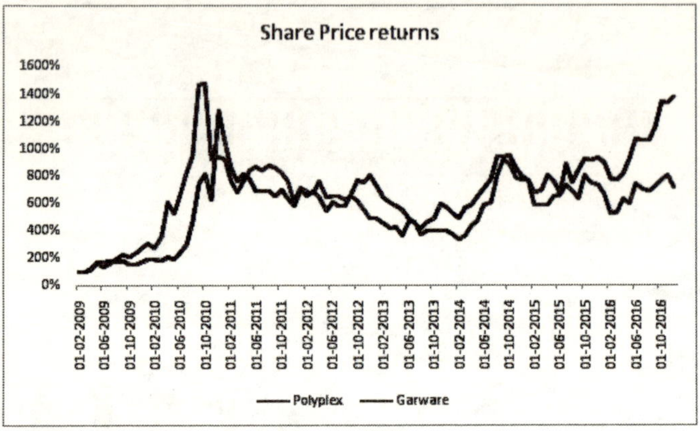

Percentage returns on stock

No matter which player in the industry one invested in during 2010-11, one would have made absolutely no returns for a very long time on these stocks. But there was a fortune to be made in 2008-09 and with increasing capacity utilisation, there were returns to be made post-2015. The signal to exit a commodity play is when multiple players are looking to increase capacity disproportionately in the industry. Similarly, industry-wide under-investment is clearly a value creator for times to come. We had earlier discussed how devastating the sugar capital subsidy scheme was for the sugar industry after 2004.

Another very important factor while playing the commodities story is to not get too enamoured by earnings multiples like P/E and EV/EBITDA, but to look at book value, replacement cost and industry capacity utilization trend very carefully. If one has to look at earnings multiples, look at an average earning of one full cycle.

In fact, one can make money on commodities cycle, by buying them at high TTM (trailing twelve months) P/E and selling at low TTM P/E. When commodities are in a bull run, often earnings move very rapidly, giving an illusion of cheapness to the stock, while trading at multiple time book value; similarly, on the down cycle, the reverse happens, and stocks look expensive because of high P/E even though they are at a significant discount to their replacement value.

Not all commodities behave in a similar fashion. Commodities in regulated sectors have their own regulatory dynamics that need to be understood. Commodities like cement, which have a large freight cost, behave differently from some of the other commodities that can easily be imported. In the earlier example of photovoltaic cell manufacturing, the value of the produce was extremely high vis-à-vis its weight, which not only made it possible to manufacture and transport all over the world, the goods could even be airlifted, cutting down delivery timelines. It was a truly global commodity. Steel as a commodity lies somewhere in between.

Another very interesting commodity play that happened in the Indian markets was with respect to graphite electrodes. Graphite electrodes are used to melt scrap in an electric arc furnace to produce new steel. Steel can be produced via iron ore through traditional blast furnaces, which typically use coal, or through steel scrap, which use electric arc furnace.

In developed markets, where the availability of steel scrap is better, there is greater use of steel scrap to create new steel. However, in emerging economies, the availability of scrap typically lags the demand and hence blast furnaces, which create steel through iron ore, are more widely used.

Somewhere in 2017, the Chinese government started to become more conscious of the adverse pollution impact of using basic oxygen furnace (BOF), and at the same time, the availability of steel scrap in China had started to increase prolifically. According to a blog on worldstreet.org, in 2016, the share of electric arc furnace (EAF) in China was only 6.5% vis-à-vis around 45% in the rest of the world.

This preferred conversion to EAF in China led to an unprecedented demand spike in graphite electrodes. One of the key raw materials for making graphite electrodes is needle coke, which also had limited supply, and the graphite electrodes companies were competing with the electric vehicles segment for needle coke. This led to a sudden demand-supply mismatch in the availability of graphite electrodes, and the prices went through the roof. From $ 1940/ tonne at the end of 2016, the price of graphite electrodes went all the way up to $ 16,130/ tonne in September of 2018 only to retrace back to $ 5,646/ tonne by end of 2019.

The fortune of the commodity price was demonstrated in profitability, and stock prices of the two major players in India, HEG and Graphite India Ltd. From a turnover of INR 903 crores in FY 17, the turnover of HEG went to INR 6,702 crores in FY 19. The EBITDA rise was even more meteoric, up from a modest INR 88 crores to a whopping INR 4,767 crores. The forever sleepy stock rose to stratospheric levels, before coming off more than 75% from their peaks.

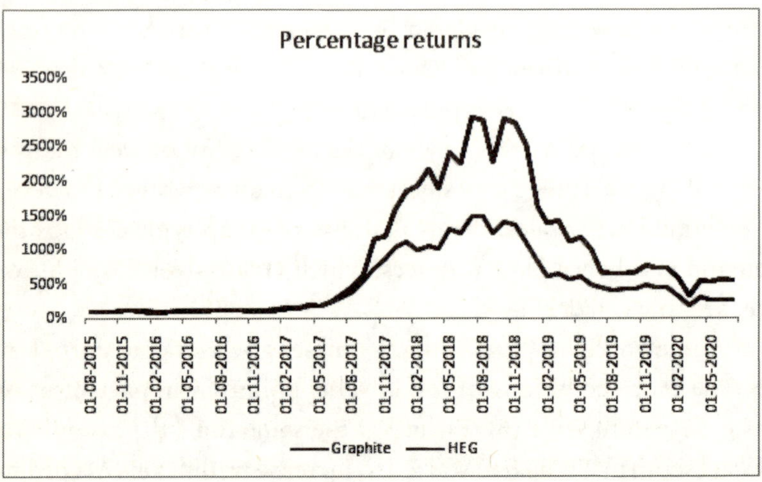

To reflect the uptick in the price of the underlying commodity, the stock also went berserk, giving 10x to 20x returns in a short span of time for those who could exit in time. Both these stocks in terms of their FY 19 earnings multiple are at extremely low P/Es but that does not make the stock any cheaper. Like we said earlier, in commodities one can make lots of money by selling at low P/Es and buying at high P/Es. The understanding that no matter how good your return on assets and margins become in the short run, at the end of the day it is a commodity that will return to its fair level over a period of time, is an important learning to help an investor in a commodity stock exit in time.

The general rule is that if the last upcycle for the commodity was too far out, the next cycle will either be sustained and longer or will have a bigger spike than the previous time. A sustained upcycle sees the surpluses being deployed for new capacity addition, and hence the demand-supply mismatch gets corrected. A large spike kind of a situation happens when the commodity in question is critical for the consumer, and fearing shortages they start stocking up. The stocking up causes further shortages and spike in prices. This starts improving the industry-wide capacity utilization and otherwise inefficient capacities also come back to start production; alternatively, the raw material prices for producing the commodity also starts spiking. This is typically followed by a period of de-stocking, regulatory interventions or both, and brings back price rationality to the market. It is often the regulatory aspects and the duties that are very difficult to predict on a sustainable basis, which makes playing the cycle on these kinds of commodities very difficult and forces the investor to have longer-term patience.

Another important category of commodity players worth studying are high-cost producers. High-cost producers are those players in the industry who have a higher cost of production for the same commodity other players can produce for lesser. In the short term often a high-cost producer can create greater value for an investor than a low-cost producer.

For simplicity sake, let us take the example of an imaginary commodity called 'gamma'. Gamma's market price in a down cycle is at INR 100/kg. Mr. A, who is a low-cost producer, can produce this at INR 70/kg, while a high-cost producer, Mr. B, can produce this at INR 90/kg. Both these companies are trading at eight times their PE. Due to an upcycle, the price of gamma increases from INR 100 to INR 130. While the gross margin for Mr. A doubles from INR 30 to INR 60, the gross margin for Mr. B quadruples from INR 10 to INR 40. This disproportionate expansion in margin often creates superior shareholder returns in the short run.

Too simplistic! Let's look at Tata Steel and SAIL during the 2005-2008 bull run.

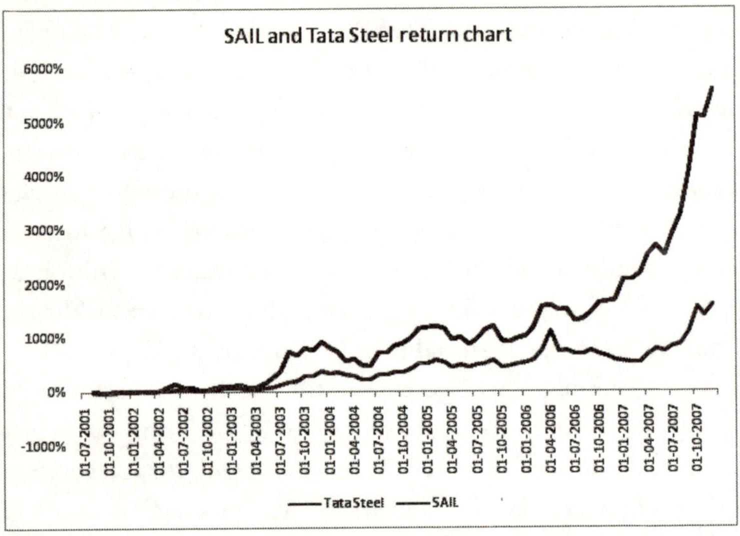

Tata Steel, which up to that point had no hangover of Corus and was one of the most efficient players in the steel industry, 'only' went 10x from the previous bear market, while SAIL went 50x from its lows. SAIL had a larger capacity but always traded at a steep discount to Tata Steel, which was seen as a more efficient producer of steel. But once steel prices started heading north, the delta it had for SAIL was multiple times that for Tata steel, and hence the crazy run in the stock price. In commodities there are periods where one can make money by betting on a slower horse.

We have talked about the risk of leverage in a commodity industry. One very interesting commodity from that perspective has been the container glass industry in India. Container glass business typically serves consumers in the beer, food consumption and pharmaceuticals industry. Around the later part of the first decade of this millennium, container glass prices in India started going up, improving the EBITDA margins to the vicinity of 20%. The business had been increasing in capital intensity and some put the size of a minimum economic size plant capex at INR 600-700 crores for a 650 tpd plant. The market leader in the space, Hindusthan National Glass (HNG), took a very aggressive capacity expansion plan of three lines, aggregating 1,950 tpd at a capex of INR 2,000 crores. The overall organized container glass industry at that time was around 5,500 tpd.

Similarly, some of the other players in the industry like HSIL also undertook capacity expansion in the industry. A large increase in supply of the product led to complete erosion of pricing power in the hands of the producers. To top it all, the borrowings more than quadrupled for HNG, increasing from INR 641 crores at the

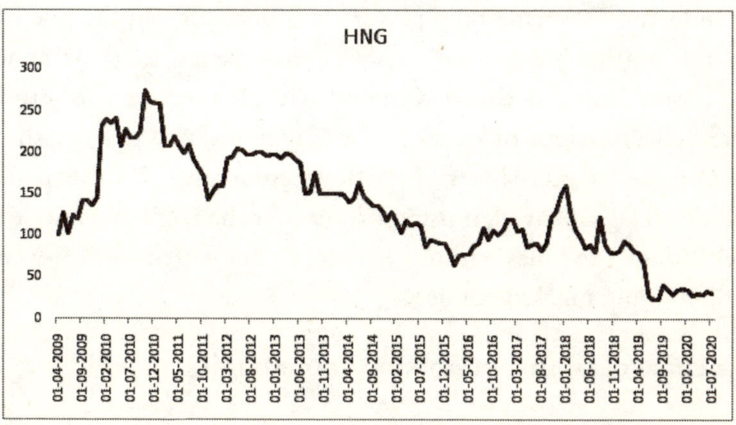

end of FY 11 to INR 2,697 crores by end of FY 14. Due to excess supply, the EBITDA margins collapsed to 9% in FY 13 and they had a large debt to repay.

Imagine the supply of a commodity that has an annualised consumption growth rate of 6-7% increase by 50% in a very short span of time and the market leader trying to do that to further gain market share and drive out competition. This is a classic recipe for disaster for all players in the industry, especially if the end user of that commodity is also a business and not a consumer. Retail consumers are often less price-sensitive than a business consumer. Larger quantities for a business consumer mean that they need to continuously optimize their costs. If as an institutional buyer of the commodity, I know that my supplier has a very low-capacity utilization, high debt levels and I have multiple options of sellers to choose from, it becomes that much easier for me to drive down a hard bargain.

The commodity prices and hence the stock prices kept crashing and the debt increasingly became unserviceable. Later, in 2019 the lenders of the market leader in container glass business took the company into bankruptcy proceedings. Probably at a time when years of underinvestment and negligible capacity addition in the industry are bringing a semblance of pricing power back in the industry. The remaining players will benefit from the upcycle, but the market leader will undergo insolvency in these times. The lesson clearly is that a commodity cycle investor needs to be extremely conscious of leverage not only in his own balance sheet, but also the balance sheets of portfolio companies. If the eventual turn of cycle is delayed, it is important that the company is able to tide through the times without eroding its net worth by the reverse compounding machine of debt.

The curse of sunrise sectors on commodities!

Sunrise sectors in their early years see a huge demand-supply mismatch for the commodities they are manufacturing. Looking at the mismatch globally, every manufacturer and investor is chasing the mirage of super-normal profits and keeps adding to capacities. Sometimes the rate of capacity addition and technology improvements in sunrise sectors is so rapid that the money lost by the entire value chain of manufacturing is back-breaking.

Let us look at what happened to solar manufacturing in the last decade and a half:

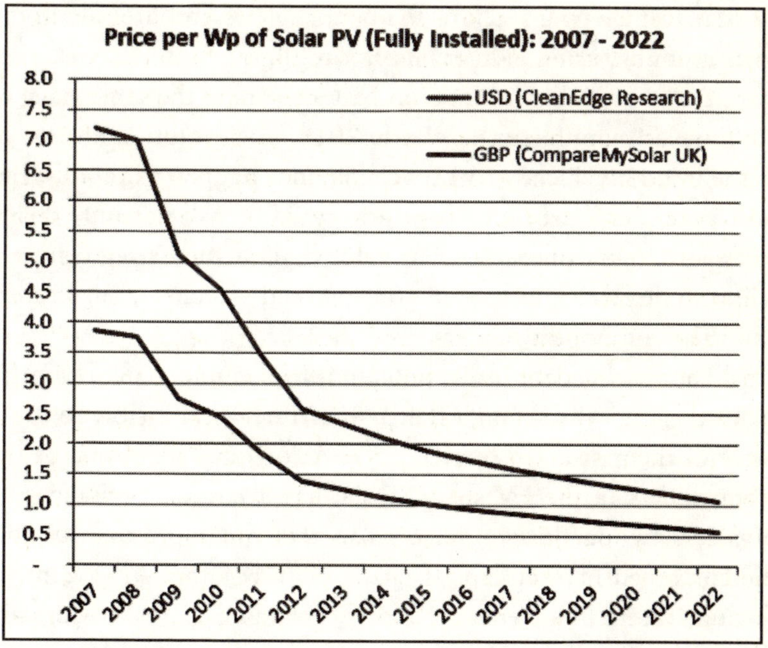

Source: renewableenergyhub.co.uk

It was the sunrise industry the world was looking at to reduce its carbon footprint and reduce dependence on coal-based thermal power. Initially, the industry was driven by subsidies in the form of capital subsidies and feed in tariffs (FITs or assured fixed tariffs by governments), where governments across the world assured a higher tariff for solar power plants to support adoption. This created a mad rush for capacity addition in many European countries and a large-scale manufacturing value chain across the world. The adoption was faster than what one had imagined, and a PV module price crashed approximately 80% in a span of a little over a decade.

While these created large utility-scale power plants in lots of large economies at a relatively economical price, what it did to manufacturers of polysilicon and photovoltaic cells was devastating. There was a joke among solar manufacturing specialists in 2011-12 that just keeping track of the bankruptcies and fire sale in the solar manufacturing industry itself is a full-time job.

Today probably lithium ion batteries are at the same stage of life as solar manufacturing was in 2010. The evolution and crash in the electric vehicles (EV) space may not happen as rapidly, but over time it will create its own graveyard. It will not only create graveyards in the manufacturing value chain of the EV segment, but will also displace and disrupt conventional vehicle manufacturers and their component makers.

The exuberance over potential frontrunners in a sunrise industry is usually so high that it is virtually impossible to get a piece of them at a reasonable price. As of June 2020, one of the frontrunners in the EV space, Tesla, has a market capitalization of $ 200 billion. Just to get a sense, this was more than double the combined market capitalization of three other American car manufacturers like General Motors, Ford and Chrysler. Cars are definitely not commodities, the example cited is just to demonstrate investor enthusiasm for the sunrise sector. Every mainstream car manufacturer, auto component company in the industry wants a slice of the EV value chain pie. As a Polycycle Investor, one would do well to follow the trends from a distance and not be lured by growth numbers and demand-supply mismatch stories one will continue to hear. Unfortunately, the incumbents who are part of the ICE engine manufacturing chain do not have that luxury. For them it is damned if you do, damned if you don't.

Non-commodity plays in commodities

While we are discussing commodities, one is reminded of one of the most esoteric commodity pulled out of thin air by the United Nations under the United Nations Framework Convention on Climate Change or (UNFCCC). This was called certified emissions reduction (CERs), popularly known as carbon credits. Under the Kyoto Protocol, signatories agreed to reduce carbon emissions, and the first phase of commitments was from the 2008-2012 period. A market for CERs was created where the polluting industries were supposed to buy CERs to the extent of carbon emissions and the industries that generated end products from substitutes, which helped in reducing carbon emissions. HFC (hydrofluorocarbon) was seen as one of the worst offenders of green-house gas emissions and one tonne of HFC reduction was valued at almost 14,800 times that of carbon dioxide. HFC is one of the key refrigerant gases that were in use in early 2000s and its elimination was seen as critical to contain ozone layer depletion.

SRF, which had an HFC incineration plant, was a major beneficiary of the carbon credit regime. However, in 2008, triggered by GFC, there was a rethink among signatories, especially developed countries that had to shoulder a larger burden of carbon reduction in the first phase, which ended in 2012. This led to serious end-use restrictions on CERs and whittled away the mandatory nature of CERs. A sunset clause for CERs was written and the prices for CERs, which were to be generated post-2012, started to collapse dramatically.

In the general market crash due to GFC, and with visibility on CER revenues post-2012 diminishing, the price of SRF crashed by more than 75%. All the way up to 2009, the company was available at less than cash plus expected CER revenue for the next three years. Effectively, their entire technical textile and specialty chemical business was available for free. Pessimism in commodities creates huge opportunities for investors as long as balance sheets are taken care of.

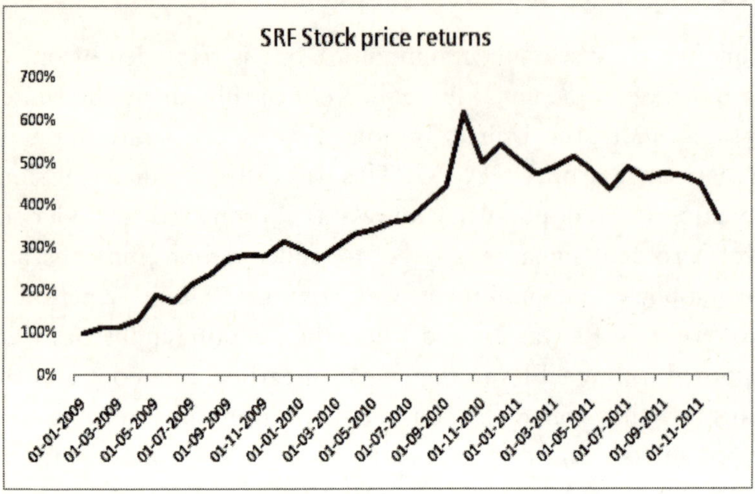

Another industrial commodity worth studying has been the refractories space. This is a relatively small industry in India, probably just about a billion dollar in size, used in industries where production requires very high temperatures. They are used to line hot surfaces to protect the metal or other surfaces from the process heat. The industry, historically, has been a fragmented one with very few players of scale and size. Around 2008, RHI from Germany came into the fray and acquired Orient Refractories and then merged their existing business with the listed Orient Refractories. Similarly, the other global player, Vesuvius India, also ramped up capacity, brought new materials and technologies, which gradually started giving them market leadership and advancement over other competitors. This clearly created a gap in market perception between the two players and other competitors, and the multiples, too, expanded for these players. In a mid-size commodity industry, if one can garner market share and access through market consolidation, value can be created for market leadership, pricing power and brand, which were hitherto absent. Such themes are always exciting and more sustainable commodity themes to play. Both these companies went on to be five to seven times between 2008 and 2018, creating tremendous value in a small B2B (business to business) commodity industry.

Some of the other products that are strictly not commodities also have commodity-like features, to the extent that the prices are largely market determined. Basmati rice is one such example. It is a very interesting commodity for a few reasons. It is known worldwide for its long grains and aroma. India has a GI (geographical indication) tag on basmati rice and only rice produced in seven northern states of India can be labeled as basmati. Further, larger players in this industry have managed to create a distribution and brand in the MENA (Middle East and North Africa) region, which helps them get a further premium over other rice brands.

With limited supply, unique positioning and increasing brand value for basmati rice, the commodity started to look more like a consumer industry. However, bulk of the market and the most lucrative market for basmati rice continued to be the middle-eastern countries. A fresh wave of sanctions on Iran by the United States in 2017 made payments from Iran difficult to obtain. Iran being one of the major importers of basmati rice, the demand kept falling.

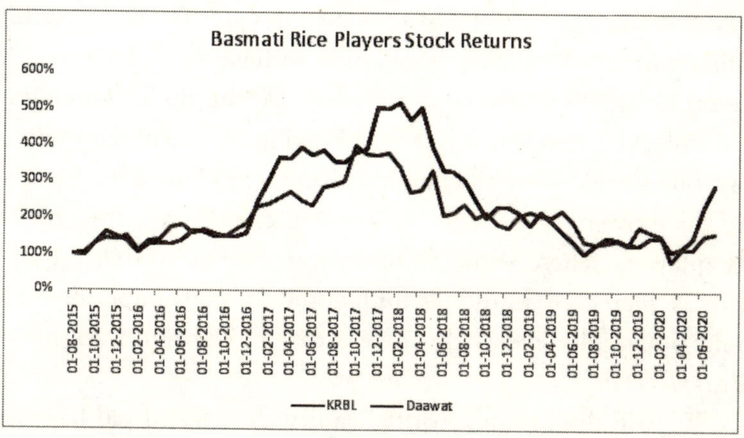

The sector, which was looking to turn the tide from being positioned as a branded consumer story, suddenly started to feel the pinch of demand squeeze. However, agriculture produce, if unregulated, has probably the smallest cycles. A year of low realization will make farmers shift to an alternative more lucrative crop. The Covid crisis is further going to impact demand and realisation. This is already leading to a shift in cropping pattern with farmers in agricultural belts of Punjab moving to cash crops like cotton and varieties of rice with a defined minimum support price (MSP). Basmati is a water-guzzling variety, and there has been a push for conservation of water. Also, large parts of north India have been suffering from acute pollution levels in winter. The burning of rice in those months further accentuates the problem, leading to either additional costs for disposing of the husk or fear of penalties.

It's difficult to say how the global situation is going to play out, but all the metrics suggest that a period of demand uptick will happen over the next 24 months or so. In commodity plays, especially commodities with lower margins and low-value addition potential, it is useful to look at net working capital movement of the companies. Increasing amount of money getting stuck in inventories and receivables is often a sign of poor quality of earnings, and reliability of the earnings. It also puts in question the ability of a company to recover receivables and further continuity of that business. Reducing receivables, with improving net working capital, is usually a sign of demand uptick and things looking up. As a Polycycle Investor if one was looking for a commodity cycle play, one should view the financial health of players in this space and the movement of their net working capital over the previous few quarters. There is the natural protection of having a GI tag, there is increased branding and domestic consumption, which could potentially even help in re-rating of the multiples for the sector overall.

We will discuss some of the sanity checks and red flags that one needs to be wary of while investing later in the book. Most of them apply to investing in commodities; probably they impact the working of a commodity company even more than some of the other industries. Agricultural commodities are very easy to sell in the market and the inventory can disappear in no time. Similarly, the sanctity of receivables is also not the same as it would be in other B2B sales, where the counter-party is often someone of greater repute. Also, in agricultural commodities one needs to understand the seasonality of the product. For instance, in the case of sugar and basmati rice, inventories are often high after the harvest season (crushing in case of sugar) and deplete over the rest of the year.

It is also important in such commodities that the investor partners with the right player and plays the right part in the value chain. Basmati rice exports, to that extent, are largely an oligopolistic market with a few players dominating the space and others playing a catch-up game. There is a significant difference in the realisation of a strong brand player vis-à-vis a new entrant, which makes the possibility of the produce graduating from being a commodity to becoming a consumer play very likely. The brand spend, advertising spend and market presence suggest that even domestic players are willing to pay a premium for a branded basmati rice pack as against an unknown brand.

Like we have discussed in multiple examples above, commodity cycle investing has very unique dynamics. Your investee company in a commodity cycle can go belly up much sooner than the eventual cycle upturn. Bankruptcies and complete erosion of capital are commonplace in the commodity space. Partially because most commodities have higher capex and typically a large number of industry players look to expand indiscriminately in an upcycle, simultaneously leading to both lower capacity utilisation and decrease in gross margins, to add leverage to the mix, the surplus available for equity shareholders can evaporate rather quickly.

Also, it is virtually impossible to develop a deep understanding of multiple commodities. Anyone looking to play the commodity cycle should try and select three to four commodities and build a deeper understanding of these cycles and players in that space.

One must also always build a buffer for a few years and be willing to take a commodity bet for a period of even five to seven years. In commodity cycles you are paid to wait – the longer the cycle takes to turn, better it is. It means that the new upcycle is due to a sustained period of under-investment in the industry. Further, if the cycle for setting up a new capacity for the commodity is longer, it is even better. The longer one has been made to wait, the greedier one should get in terms of timing the exit. While playing a commodity, it is extremely important to have time as your ally. One must be willing to hold on to a stock for years together with no performance and exit when the company is in the best of its financial health and is having super-normal profits.

In an upcycle there is always a lot of noise about why the cycle is going to sustain, reasons like more end-user demand, shortage of raw material, consolidation of pricing power etc. Typically, such noise is there because corporates, bankers and analysts are all incentivised to say so, to enable fund raise for the new project the big boys in the industry are looking to fund. Timing the exit for a commodity stock is an art. Generally, announcements of large capex are a signal to unwind positions. The bigger the announcements, the faster one should unwind. It is tricky because you do not want to exit too soon on a position you have held for multiple years; at the same time, you don't want to be left holding a debt-ridden overpriced stock when the tide turns.

5

Product Life Cycle

Unlike the other cycles we discussed earlier, a product cycle is not like a self-repeating wave. They are longer term and often have one rise, one fall and then may disappear altogether. Different products have a different product lifecycle; while the staples and consumption goods have a more stable lifecycle curve, technology products and utilitarian products have a more finite life.

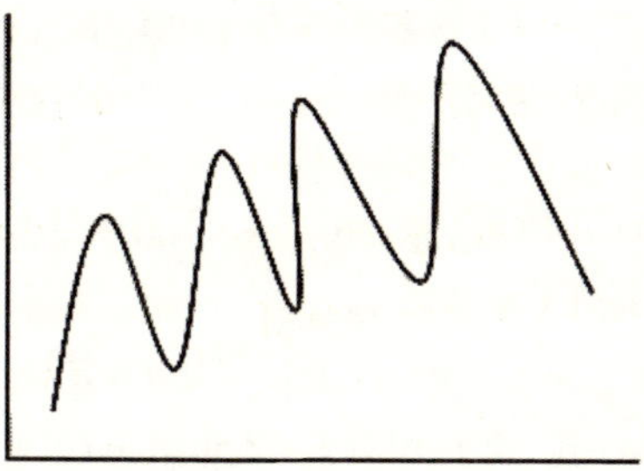

Figure A.

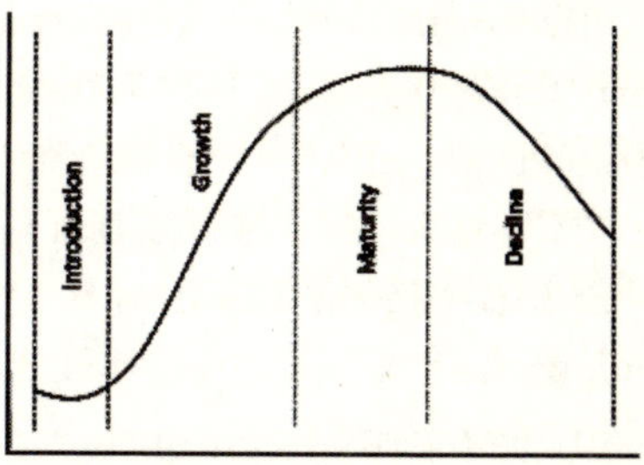

Figure B.

While market cycles and commodity cycles often look like the figure on the left, with repeated ups and downs and generally trending upwards, product cycles mostly look like Figure B. on the right, with a slow introduction stage where a market is being created, a rapid growth stage as product acceptance increases, a moderate growth maturity stage and an eventual decline. The length of each phase may change from product to product and industry to industry, but most products which do take off typically have a lifecycle as mentioned above.

In the technology space the lifecycle may be very different, with a sharper growth and sharper fall from the cliff, while products meant for personal consumption, like edibles and cosmetics, have a much longer lifecycle. For instance, soap will have a much longer lifecycle, spanning over centuries, as against a technology product like a camera, television or a mobile phone. The television industry in the last three decades has already transitioned from CRT (cathode ray tube) and LCD (liquid crystal display) to LED (light emitting diode) technology. Even within LED televisions, the standard definition and high definition televisions are going obsolete at a very rapid rate, with the industry moving to ultra high definition smart televisions. Similarly, Nokia, which at one point was the bestselling phone in India and in large parts of the world, started to face trouble with the advent of smart phone. Blackberry, which was the gold standard for business phones and a status symbol, has also had a tough run post the advent and proliferation of touch screen phones. However, it's unlikely that corn flakes or soap will either decline or get extinguished as a product in such short spans.

When investing in a business, it is important to understand what lifecycle the business is in and the obsolescence risk one is undertaking. While doing this, it is important to define the industry relatively narrowly. For instance, while the solar PV (photovoltaic) business took off and grew at a phenomenal rate in the last decade, some of the alternative technologies, like CSP (concentrated solar power, popularly known as solar thermal) and technologies using rare earth materials to produce solar power, lost out completely. That typically does not always happen with consumer products; even though aerated drinks may get wildly popular, fruit juices will continue to have their own consumers and vice versa.

Most construction material and building material will fall

somewhere in between. Engineered wood (like veneers, ply and boards) may increasingly take market share from natural wood, and tiles may take market share from natural stone, and brass faucets may make way for zinc and chrome-plated plastic, but these changes are usually much slower and take decades to get culturally adopted.

While investing in a business it is worthwhile to dig deep into the business we are investing in, understand the product lifecycle and ability of the company to repurpose it. It is also important to understand potential substitutes for the product that we are investing in. Market space disruptions need to be understood in great depth.

Technology-led disruptions recurring at an increasing pace

Like products, services have their own lifecycle. Ride hailing services like Easycab and Meru (popularly known as radio cabs), which were ubiquitous in Indian urban centers and were upgrading the taxi experience for consumers in these metros, were in for a rude shock when mobile app-based ride hailing services like Uber and Ola started to become popular. Instead of investing their capital in acquiring new cars, these mobile app-based services started investing in acquiring customers and getting drivers hooked to their platform. The ride costs for the customers came down by more than a half and customer experience improved dramatically. The amount of money drivers were making in those early years would have been impossible for them to even dream of.

While a lot of the growth for these app-based ride hailing companies came by using up the equity money they raised from large private equity funds, there was an inherent advantage they had. As a customer, one did not book his cab well in advance and it was available on a real-time basis. One could track exactly where the driver was and his route was mapped. Directions were automatically given by the app and the payment directly deducted. Apart from this, there was a huge saving angle. Based on anecdotal evidence, the percentage of billed ride increased from 40% for radio cabs to 70% in app-based services. Even when these cabs moved to charging customers more and paying drivers less, the old model of radio cab had no chance of making a real comeback because of product superiority and efficiency.

The same trend of large aggregators and digital intermediaries disintermediating multiple businesses is a trend that is here to stay. Airline bookings, hotel bookings and real estate brokerage are some of the industries where the brick and mortar form is losing market share very rapidly to digital players. The same is happening in financial services.

Relatively new broker Zerodha, which started operations in 2010, is already the largest broker in the country, well ahead of its incumbent peers, including those backed by major banks like ICICI and HDFC. According to a news report, as of June 2019, Zerodha had 9.8 lakh active clients, as against 8.8 lakh active clients for ICICI Securities and 6.5 lakh clients for HDFC Securities. While the fee income share will not be similar, the disruption is real. Other players like Upstox and 5paisa are also playing the discount brokerage game and upsetting the applecart for incumbents. Mutual fund distribution is also getting disrupted the same way and even strong incumbent intermediaries are forced to offer direct plans with zero brokerage.

The amount of money being spent on payments and with platforms like UPI, low-cost payment gateway like RuPay and some of the other QR code-based low-cost models for fintech companies will sooner rather than later impact merchant's preference for some of these models. The merchant fee for credit card payments on Visa, Mastercard and American Express varies between 1% and 2.5% from merchant to merchant, while the new-age models pretty much cost nothing.

The global automobile agency is also going through a wave of disruption with the spectre of electric vehicles, autonomous driving and shared mobility likely to disrupt the industry in multiple waves over the next couple of decades. However, the pace of change in the automobile industry is expected to be slower than those in services. Building an automobile business requires a whole new eco-system to develop, with quality auto component players, distribution channel, fuel retailing infrastructure and large dollops of capital.

It is not only the car itself that will change, even the entire car selling experience and infrastructure are changing. Car distributorships will also face challenges from online selling of cars. There was a time there was a proliferation of mobile retailing formats in the country. These stores offered a variety of brands and phones to choose from. However, the e-commerce space completely disrupted it, and in the next wave all these retail formats increasingly started to become financially unviable and started to close down. Sooner or later the automobile industry will also face the same disruption.

The Indian multi-brand retail industry has FDI (foreign direct investment) restrictions and foreign players cannot directly play in this industry. This has forced even e-commerce players in the country to work as marketplaces and not as a full-fledged retailer. A marketplace is where the seller allows other sellers to market their product on its platform, without themselves taking the onus of selling or owning the inventory. In spite of that, brick and mortar retail is seeing a wave of disruption and increasingly more and more segments of the industry are getting displaced by e-commerce. Books, grocery, mobile, electronics, home furnishing, stationery retail, all are slowly but surely losing market share to e-commerce. The United States has been seeing a wave of bankruptcies in organised brick and mortar retail space; retail majors like J.C Penney, Aldo, Neiman Marcus and almost a dozen other retailers filed for bankruptcy in the first half of 2020 alone.

Democratisation of access to capital

The pace of disruption in the world has accelerated dramatically over the last couple of decades. The importance of understanding the lifecycle of a product has never been more pronounced as it is in the 21st century. The segments we want to play, the multiples we should be willing to pay, are all dependent on our view on the length of the lifecycle of the product, its current stage and the disruptions it may face in the coming years. Monopolistic or oligopolistic businesses, large brand businesses built with years of efforts, to build brands, distribution capabilities and vendors are being upended by newbies with amazing regularity. Entrepreneurship is getting democratised at a rapid pace and access to capital is no more centered around islands of large corporates.

The threat of disruption for large corporates is so high that even these large corporates are increasingly getting their own family offices and treasuries to invest in these disruptive technologies to stay updated and have a finger in the pie. In 1998, Yahoo had the option to buy Google for a princely sum of $ 1 million. In 2002 they had another option to buy Google for $ 5 billion, but Yahoo turned down the offer on both occasions. Probably the costliest miss in the history of global M&A (mergers and acquisitions). In 2020, Alphabet, the company that owns Google, had a market capitalisation of close to $1 trillion and Yahoo is a very pale shadow of what it used to be.

It would have taken a very brave man to predict such a stunning reversal of fortunes for the two tech majors. As a student of lifecycle of products, one may prefer a company in a decline stage but with a longer runaway ahead vis-à-vis an industry in the middle of such disruptions.

Mostly high-growth sunrise industries trade at very high multiples and yet one runs a very high risk of betting on the wrong horse. We know how Tesla, one of the frontrunners, is valued more than twice the combined market cap of the next three American automobile companies. But there are at least another half a dozen companies worldwide who have made significant progress in the EV space. Also, who knows if the next wave of autonomous driving happens sooner rather than later? It may throw up completely new leaders.

Changes in the automotive industry are likely to result in large-scale bankruptcies over the next two decades all across the value chain. This will not only include OEMs (original equipment manufacturers) but also the auto-component players and distribution channels. However, even these large-scale disruptions may present the opportunity of a lifetime. While the multiples of the entire legacy of the automotive industry may come down, some of the verticals with a lower rate of disruption may actually grow stronger while trading at lower multiples.

Identifying industries with lower rate of disruption

The manufacturers of low-tech items in the automotive space may be better off. The manufacturers of plastic parts, the metal recycling companies and automotive lighting companies may actually benefit from this disruption. Some of the other auto-component companies that are more diversified will have to dabble in new technology, and the space may be vacated by smaller players. Larger auto-component players may actually end up consolidating their market share. For OEMs, too, there will be little incentive to try and get into the complete auto-component ecosystem themselves, and they may find very little merit in trying to do the manufacturing of low-tech items themselves.

We have already seen that happen in the solar manufacturing chain. Where the high-tech players with larger capital intensity had bankruptcies, but low-tech players like module makers and system integrators continued to grow. In the solar value chain, making poly silicon, wafers and cells were probably the highest value-add items and required state-of-the-art machinery. Making modules and doing system integration were relatively easier jobs and did not involve a large capex. There is virtue in choosing to do simpler things than trying to do technologically complex business, especially if you have to pay a hefty price for a rapidly evolving technology which others can also buy in the marketplace.

As a thumb-rule, the part of the value chain with a very high capex intensity and susceptible to technology upgradation is the worst part of the value chain to be in unless one owns the technology. Often players in this space are forced to sell their produce on variable cost basis and there is very little pricing power or ability to recover capital cost. The changes in technology further reduce the ability to recover costs over a longer term as newer companies are able to buy more efficient machines at a lesser cost.

This is the reason consumer products and brands enjoy the kind of premium they enjoy. Their product lifecycles are extremely long and the capital intensity is extremely low. This allows these businesses to consistently throw surplus cash flows. To top that, there is a natural affinity of the end consumer for the brand, which allows stronger brands to price their produce at a premium to a new competitor. A certain degree of technological change may actually help some of the companies by continuously weeding out smaller unorganised players who struggle to keep on re-investing in their businesses.

While looking at the rate of technological change, one must also assess the size of the industry itself. The larger the size of the industry, greater the incentive for either a new player or, for that matter even an incumbent to deploy large pools of capital to disrupt the industry to gain market share.

Even in e-commerce, a player has a better chance if he works in a niche and builds competencies around that niche rather than trying to play the larger plays. An Info Edge (naukri.com), which focused on jobs listing, matrimonial sites, B2B listing platforms like IndiaMART, furniture specialists like Pepperfry, have competed better with the big e-retailers than the likes of ShopClues and Snapdeal.

How disruptions snowball

The advent of a smartphone triggered the decline of many industries. The smartphone became your time-keeper, camera, notepad, music player all rolled into one. It not only played music, but could also store and stream music. The portable music industry could never revive from this onslaught. CD players and the walkman disappeared in virtually no time. The portable camera is facing a similar crisis, as the quality of camera on the smartphone keeps getting better. According to Statista, the sales of standalone digital camera dropped by a whopping 87% in the decade starting 2010. The industry for camera rolls, of course, died a long time back. The dark room and the film developing services also exist mostly in the folklores of a bygone era.

It is extremely important to spot these trends early on, as typically these changes happen early on in a trickle and then it pours. OTT (over the top) content providers are likely to be similarly disruptive for a lot of products. While the demand for smart TVs will increase, it is creating a moment of truth for conventional television channels. The consumer has been given the liberty to pick the time and the content he wants to watch. Streaming on the internet is making the direct to home (DTH) service providers sweat. The country's broadband penetration is still relatively low, but more evolved markets like the US have already seen television advertising revenue trending south since 2016. As broadband penetration in India increases, similar trends are expected to replicate here too. Even production houses that somewhat enjoyed the privileges of a robust distribution or equity with channels, may be made to re-evaluate their business models as anyone with the ability to create good content may find it possible to put it on an online platform. The fight for prime-time slots and premium put on top star cast to that extent will stand reduced.

Some of the other industries that may get impacted by OTT platforms are the movie exhibition business, although they are not direct competitors and provide a very different experience of going out and a bigger screen. However, as the television screen sizes and quality of content keep getting better, one would think the frequency with which a patron visits a movie theater may come down over a period of time. While movie exhibition might still continue to be a great business, one will want to be careful about the multiples one would want to pay for them. It is difficult to imagine that the movie exhibition business in the next two decades will grow at the same pace it grew in the first two decades of the century.

Obsolescence in some of industries is not as painful to adapt to as it is in others. The humble lighting industry has also seen its own share of obsolescence over the last two decades. The industry first started moving from the conventional incandescent lights to CFL (compact fluorescent lamps) and mid-way through that transition, the industry started moving to LED (light emitting diode) technology. The energy savings on moving from incandescent lights to LED were over 90% of the conventional incandescent bulbs. However, like it happens with most technologies, the cost per unit was much higher. With some policy interventions and innovative business models, the adoption started to ramp up relatively quickly and has pretty much made the other two alternatives, incandescent lights and CFLs, redundant. In spite of this rapid obsolescence, the stronger incumbents were not impacted disproportionately, as the business was built on both brand and distribution. Capex intensity in the business was also relatively low, allowing the transition to be smooth.

If one has to look at what are the differences between why the portable music players' industry died but the lighting players continued to flourish in spite of the obsolescence of their earlier products, one would come across a few very important differences. The lighting industry product switch had a very low capital intensity and the facilities for incandescent lights could partially be used for making LED lights. Further, the strength of brand and distribution gave the incumbents a head-start over any new player trying to disrupt the industry. Also, unlike a smartphone, which was being bought for a different purpose and virtually gave the music storage and streaming feature as an incidental benefit, an

LED light was only a like to like replacement. It is difficult to survive when your product becomes just an additional feature in a product for which a consumer in his mind is really not paying for. What chance would a calculator or a road map have of being as commonplace in domestic households as they were at the turn of the millennium? Similarly, the typewriter industry had no fighting chance when word processing was just one of the incidental things your home computer could do.

Not all disrupted companies are destined to die

Another very interesting example from the building material products business is the asbestos one. Asbestos used to be a preferred roofing solution for a large section of the lower middle class population in India. HIL, with its brand Charminar, was one of the prominent players in the industry. However, due to adverse health effects of asbestos, the product was banned by the Supreme Court in 2011. The profits of HIL fell from INR 61 crores in FY 13 to a mere INR 7 crores in FY 14.

Looking at the regulatory death of asbestos-based products, the company was able to come up with alternative materials for the roofing segment. They now make fibre cement sheets and coloured steel sheets for roofing solutions, to cater to the same target segment and leverage on their existing brand and distribution. They also diversified into other building material solutions like AAC (autoclaved aerated concrete) blocks, boards, insulation materials, wall putty and PVC. In 2018, to further diversify itself from a declining usage of potentially hazardous fibre cement sheets and to create a more advanced product portfolio, HIL acquired a European engineered wood flooring company called Parador. The relevance of these examples from an investor perspective is to highlight that with other strengths like distribution and brand and access to end consumers, it is often possible to re-invent oneself with new product lines. A high variable cost of production and a low capital cost are usually an ally of the incumbent.

Recycled lead is one industry that fits the bill quite well in this context. Again, because of health and environmental issues associated with lead, there is a thrust to use more and more recycled lead. By the end of 2019, almost 75% of all lead consumed in India was recycled lead. The largest user segment for the commodity has been the automotive and inverter battery segment. Telecom and solar are new-age sectors that need power back-up and storage requirements and are further fueling the demand for lead. Electric two-wheelers and e-rickshaws are also generating new demand.

Gravita, one of the top players in the lead recycling space, has been one of the major beneficiaries of this change in the industry. The decline of primary lead capacity and industry shifting from unorganised to organised has given a huge fillip to the industry. From an INR 46 crores turnover in FY 2008, Gravita had a turnover of over INR 1,200 crores in FY 2019. They have ventured into new geographies and have added aluminum recycling and plastic recycling to their product portfolio. They have also forward integrated their lead recycling business by providing turnkey solutions, lead recycling processes and plants.

However, being a commodity, it is not immune to product cycles. Let us look at their long-term price chart.

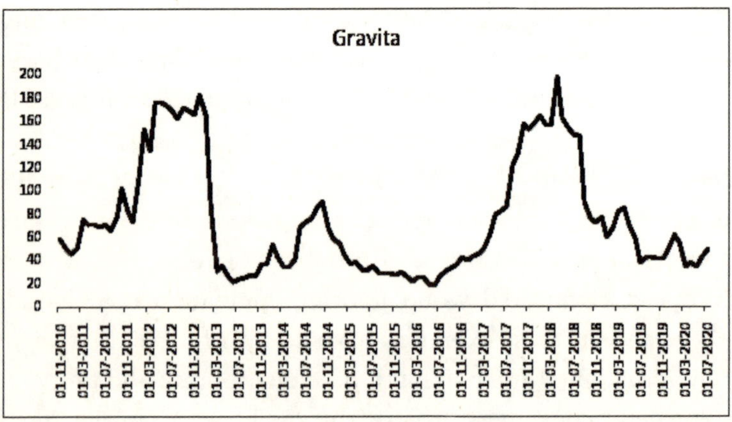

The cyclical nature of the business is there to be seen. But what is fantastic about this business is its relatively low capital intensity and low margins. The total gross block in the business was only INR 159 crores to generate a turnover of INR 1,242 crores, an asset turnover of 8x. However, the EBITDA margins in the business have consistently been in single digits. Who would want to get into such a low-margin business, with commodity risk, working capital risk and environment risks? Having an understanding of these commodities and the ability to exit and enter at the right time is a huge superpower, which can help investors beat the so-called long-term secular compounders hands down. A lot of these compounders, whose track record and value creation we keep hearing about, also suffer from a strong survivorship bias. Many stocks that were supposed to be multi-decade compounders have been anything but a compounder.

It may sound counter-intuitive to much of investor wisdom, but a low margin with a high asset turnover is a fantastic entry barrier to have. A low margin ensures that new entrants have very limited ability to get into the business and gain market share. They thrive and maintain their industry leadership position largely because their profitability is dependent on only a sliver of the whole revenue.

The fall in lead prices in 2018 has had a pronounced impact on the operating margins of Gravita and an even more pronounced impact on its stock price. As a commodity and a product cycle investor, the inherent margin of safety in this opportunity is huge.

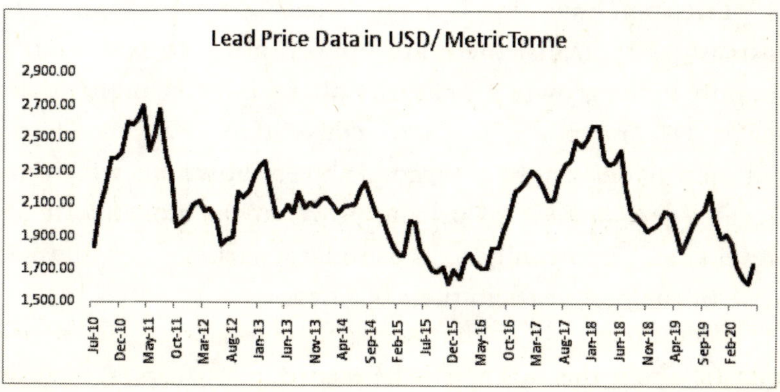

To get an opportunity to invest in an ever-growing recycling industry at 10-year-old prices with an industry leader that has demonstrated the ability to grow and diversify without having too much capital expenditure! If it were a fancier consumer sector or a sunrise stock like solar or electric vehicles, this business would have been trading at very different multiples. However, with low leverage levels and consistent growth track records, this stock is destined to be a multi-bagger like it was in the previous two upcycles. The price of lead (primary) has also started to retrace from its historical lows. The stock has everything that a classical value investor would like: moat, margin of safety, historically low multiples and free cash flows. Although the P/E on last year earnings may look high, if one looks at a five-year average PAT of the company, the P/E is less than 2x. Like we discussed in the previous chapter, one can make lot of money in commodities buying at high TTM P/Es and selling at low TTM P/Es.

If one is willing to scratch beyond the surface and find sectors that are not always in the news, not covered extensively by research analysts, the rewards can be phenomenal. A well-tracked commodity like cement or steel may not give such opportunities to buy a market leader at such mouthwatering prices, but some of the other sectors that are not mainstream provide that many more opportunities to discover hidden mispriced gems.

Life-cycle investing is a very exciting way to learn about businesses. Typically, there are opportunities to make money not only in the growth or maturity phase, but also in the decline phase. Decline phase leads to consolidation in the market and increasingly more and more players bow out, which may actually give periods of pricing power to incumbents. It also presents an opportunity to consolidate market share and have some of the best years in their business.

Let us look at Jagran Prakashan, the largest Hindi-language newspaper publication in the country. Admittedly, an industry clearly in a decline phase globally, and probably going to witness the same in the near future in India as well. *Dainik Jagran,* their flagship newspaper, had 7.3 crores readers, according to the Indian Readership Survey done in Q4 of 2019.

Jagran Prakashan has over the years widened its reach and product portfolio and is increasingly becoming stronger on the digital platform and has multiple FM (city radio stations) channels in its bouquet. The operating margin of Jagran Prakashan is one of the best in the industry.

Newspaper as a product has a positive bias towards industry leaders. They attract best talent, their surpluses allow them to have better and more content and they can invest in better newsprint also. By improving the quality of their own newspaper, one can seriously queer the pitch for the competition.

Hence, any decline in overall newspaper readership is more likely to impact the health of the weaker players, leading to further consolidation in the industry. The rate of decline for newspapers is expected to be relatively slow as increasing prosperity and literacy are going to add to readership. Admittedly, some of the advertisement spend budget of larger corporates may be taken away by digital marketing channels.

Due to Covid-19, advertisement spends done on print media and other segments have taken a backseat and there is a visible impact on their businesses. Clearly, strong players in this space are expected to get stronger and the business case for the weaker players is expected to get further strained over the next few quarters.

Jagran Prakashan at the end of FY 20 was debt-free and

had returned over INR 1,100 crores to its shareholders in the form of dividend and buy-backs in the previous three years.

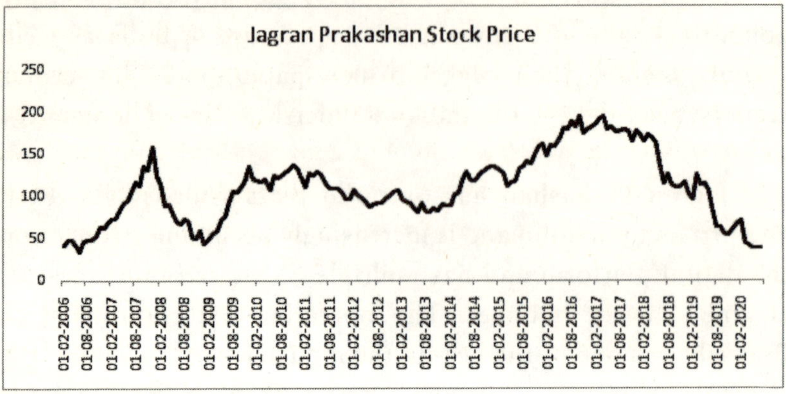

The market capitalisation of the company is almost equal to the amount it has paid back to its shareholders over the last three years. Dividend yield on a TTM basis is at over 8%.

Clearly, FY 21 will be very different from FY 20, but as a lifecycle investor, one would think that the market leader with a strong balance sheet may actually turn out stronger from this and the pandemic is unlikely to impact its permanent earning capability. A product lifecycle investor who understands these dynamics may be better off looking at such misplaced bets available in the market, rather than looking into the rear-view mirror to see what has generated returns in the near past.

Understanding the lifecycle of a product does not mean writing off everything that is in the decline phase. It only means being conscious of its impact on every player in the market, and pricing the bets rightly. Decline of an industry can often create strong monopolies for those who survive.

Being conscious of lifecycles gives an additional tool in the hands of the investor to project future growth and earnings. In the absence of these tools, one is often inclined to project past growth and margins into the future. It also forces one to think of the threat of substitutes and disruption in the industry.

The Indian stock market is a stock picker's delight. There are over 6,500 companies listed on the NSE and the BSE, and the NSE had 1,790 companies that were traded in FY 20. But if one goes beyond the 200 top companies, the market capitalisation dips below even INR 10,000 crores. Most institutional brokerages and investors are reluctant to play the turf below that. The space has jewel companies which are dominant market leaders in their own space and have strong entry barriers and market presence. Many of these players also have an enviable track record of performance and growth.

To be able to pick market leaders in a relatively small-size industry when they are mispriced and unrecognised is a very rewarding exercise. Because of their single business focus, they are usually relatively easier businesses to understand and value. This is the space where multi-baggers will be found. However, this is also the space which is away from media and institutional investors' glare and, hence, the propensity of promoters to play foul and take unscrupulous actions to the detriment of minority shareholders is that much higher.

A focus on hygiene factors like track record, income distribution and leverage becomes that much more important in the mid-cap space. One must also be willing to accept that there will be times when in spite of the diligence, we will end up getting trapped with a wrong promoter or a promoter who makes wrong capital allocation decision. But at a portfolio level, the hunt for multi-baggers is extremely rewarding even if one goes wrong on a couple of stocks.

Imagine investing in two stocks – one goes one-fifth, the other goes five times over three years. You would still make a cool 37% CAGR. One of the most underrated joys of being a long-only investor is that your downside is limited to 100% while your upside is unlimited. You will find lot of investors who put a target price to their stocks at the stage of investing, linking it to desired returns, rather than having a view on how much is the opportunity underpriced. As an investor, one needs to be careful that we do not self-cap our returns. Building an understanding of businesses and cycles allows them to have a better sense of what multiples and values should look across cycles and be able to time their exits much better. Finding a good stock to invest in is only half the battle, the long-term portfolio returns are heavily dependent on when to enter and when to exit. The 'forever' holding period is an anathema for a Polycycle Investor. Each business has its own dynamics and will have own unique holding periods.

6

Demographic Cycle

The demographic cycle is a macro-economic cycle that helps one in predicting the trends in some industries more accurately. The primary components of a demographic cycle that have a significant bearing on businesses and, in turn, on stock prices are i) age profile of population ii) income levels of population iii) education levels of population iv) the governing laws and enabling infrastructure a nation enjoys. A country like India, with a young population, a healthy GDP growth and a democratic form of governance, is a great place to be in and provides a good runway of growth. As against that a younger population with dictatorships and poor rule of law will generally continue to have civil unrests, adversely impacting businesses and investor climate. Communism in its own way can destroy economies through perpetuation of a form of governance and propping up of crony capitalists for decades together.

The governance risk

Despotic leaders of various nations have led their countries into global isolation to protect their reign and power. This has led to sanctions by other developed countries and multilateral agencies, pushing those countries into a trap of hyperinflation, wars and civil unrest. Typically, environments like these lead to a long-term value destruction for the broader markets as a whole. As an investor who looks to invest in multiple markets, it is extremely important to understand the risks they are taking with respect to the demographic nature of the country.

Communism and dictatorship often create a crony-capitalistic regime, making it virtually impossible for smaller independent business to flourish and grow in an open, equal-opportunity environment. Good businesses that you back may often be at the receiving end of the cronies and may face environmental challenges or even be outlawed. Even though there will be periods of high return for many businesses, there is always a risk lurking around the corner. The risk of the unknown, the risk of nationalisation, the risk of expropriation and the risk of rapid currency devaluation.

The risks for a multi-decade investor with large exposures to these markets are likely to end in an accident. It is extremely important for a multi-nation investor to have a view on various economies to decide his country allocation strategy and have an idea of the red flags of investing in certain geographies.

Look at Zimbabwe in 1997. The country's GDP moved from $ 9 billion to about $ 4.8 billion in a span of 10 years. The rate of hyper inflations was so high that Zimbabwe dropped 25 zeros (yes, 25 zeros!) from their currency in that period over three devaluations of their currency. For a foreign investor it would have been a nightmarish ride, completely eroding the value of his entire portfolio in Zimbabwe.

Iran, another country with global sanctions, lost half the value of its currency rial and plunged below 40,000 rials to a dollar in 2018, depreciating by over 30%. The stock exchange in its local currency has been up but as a foreign investor, getting any returns was virtually impossible. To add to that, the imposition of sanctions by the US made taking out money difficult.

India also has had its own tryst with socialism and expansionary fiscal policies. Almost invariably it led to a rapid currency devaluation, inflation and loss of investor confidence. In 1961 1 US dollar was at INR 4.76 for a dollar and India was a pegged currency. All the way through 1991, India was growing at a sub-potential growth rate of little over 4%. In 1991, India ushered in reforms, devalued the currency and allowed partial foreign currency convertibility. During 1973-74, the country's marginal rate of tax shot up to an unbelievable 97.5% and the period of emergency followed. The same was progressively brought down to 40% by 1991. While initially the industry was afraid of foreign investment drowning them, over a period this created huge opportunities and wealth for the country. Since then we have been moving towards a more progressive tax system, both on the direct and indirect tax front. The CAGR GDP growth since 1991 has been over 6.3% over a much larger base. The depth and trust in Indian markets have deepened.

However, even in the last decade, the country had an extended experience where allegations of crony capitalism in allocation of resources coupled with high fiscal deficit and inflation led to a flight of foreign investors. The Indian currency crashed from INR 46 to a dollar in 2010 to INR 65 to a dollar in September 2013. The BSE Sensex during the same period virtually consistently hovered from 17,500 to 20,000. While investors could have made rupee returns on the Indian market, the crash in currency was so steep that foreign investors were badly burnt.

There is often talk around ignoring the larger macro picture and be super focused on the positions you hold. That statement can at best be only partially true. To argue that a country or a company will continue to grow despite or in spite of any kind of government is having a very limited world-view and understanding of how governments can destroy businesses and the economy in a relatively short period of time.

The preponderance of the United States in most of the investing literature has accentuated the bias, as it has had a very long run with a growing economy, favourable population demographics through their immigration policy and with a status of reserve currency for US dollar, it has been able to sustain economic growth and shareholder value creation like no other country. This is one of the things that this book looks to address and help investors view each economy with an independent lens.

A prime example of how things can go wrong in recent times is that of Turkey. Turkey, which was vying to be seen as a liberal quasi-European country, became a virtual dictatorship in 2014. After being prime minister for three terms, ***Recep Tayyip Erdogan*** ran for presidency and won the presidential elections in 2014. However, his 2014 campaign was very different from his previous terms and, one may argue, based on evidence in public domain that it was probably a manufactured win, achieved by using the might of government machinery against opponents and detractors.

A friend of the western world, a NATO ally (a strategic alliance consisting of mostly developed western countries), which was seen as a progressive model for the Islamic world to follow and also as a bridge to the Middle East, started to become unrecognisable thereafter. The GDP of Turkey reduced from $ 950 billion in 2014 on a PPP (purchasing power parity) basis to $ 771 billion in a span of five years, consistently showing negative growth rates. The Turkish lira, which used to sell for 40 US cents, now sells for 15 US cents. One can afford to be oblivious to such trends only at their own peril and that of their portfolio.

One of the great superpowers of a Polycycle Investor is the willingness to sit on cash and cash equivalents for an extended period of time. Even while sitting on cash, it is important that the value of our exposure is not being degraded by inflation or adverse movements in currency. Knowing the currency in which you hold your cash and cash equivalents is extremely important.

Impact of age profile and income levels

Another very important aspect of demography is the age of the population. Japan, which was seen as a miracle economy in the 1970s and 1980s, started to suffer from high base effect and the ageing-population syndrome.

By no stretch of imagination was Japan actually doing badly in the post-1980s era. A high-income economy ultimately will hit a ceiling, beyond which growth does start getting moderated. Generally, somewhere around $ 20,000 is when the growth starts to moderate even for better performing economies. Japan had an additional disadvantage of slowing population growth. Somewhere in the 1970s, the population growth of Japan started to trend below 1%, and from 2011 onwards there was a negative growth in population. This is further coupled with an increase in life expectancy, which means a population aging quite rapidly. Nothing demonstrates the impact of an ageing population better than the graph below.

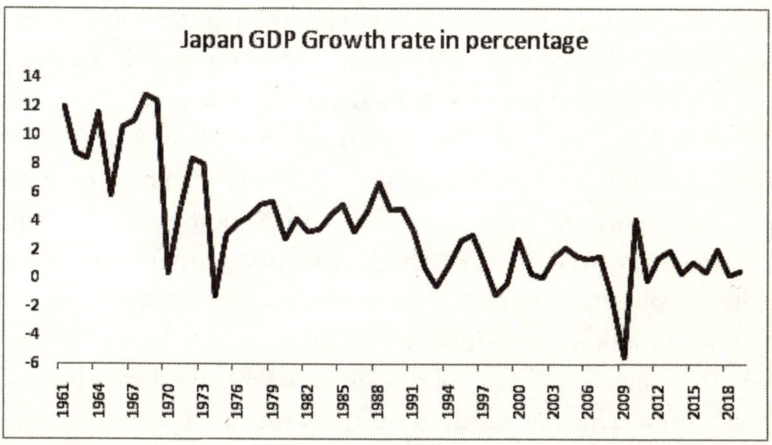

Japan GDP growth rate trend in percentage, Source: Worldbank

Nikkei Stock exchange. Logarithmic scale

A country, which is democratic, has managed to keep itself aloof from any major wars and has provided its countrymen an ever-improving quality of life, has given a negative absolute return of 33% over a long period of 30 years. Being a passive index investor in an economy like this would have been a disaster. We are not saying that individual companies in Japan have not created shareholder value or that a flattening GDP is necessarily an evil.

I have a very interesting theory; that a poor country (say PPP of $ 3,000 or less) and rich countries (PPP of $ 20,000 or more) should have a socialism bias, while mid-income economies should get more and more capitalist. Poor economies need welfare economics and need to provide basics like food, clothing and shelter to its people. Richer countries have to protect the environment from degradation and exploitation. An ever-increasing thirst for increasing income of its people creates more income disparities and social unrest. The state needs to start stepping in to provide a social cover in terms of health, education and basic livelihood. I think some of the Scandinavian countries with their high tax rates of over 50% have found the right balance. There is enough incentive for enterprise, and there is enough money that governments collect to reduce income disparities. Mid-income economies, on the other hand, need the capitalists to have enough surpluses to be able to keep re-investing in the economy to build capacities. It is important to grow the GDP and have enough surplus to be able to redistribute. Mindless GDP growth aspirations can often adversely impact the environment, resources and livelihoods of a larger population. However, socialism should only permeate the economic policy-making; the effect of communism seeping into governance style is often catastrophic.

India in a demographic sweet spot

Other important aspects of the demographic data are earnings level and savings rate. Though India continues to be a low-income economy, with a per capital GDP on an absolute basis of $ 2,000, on a PPP (purchasing power parity) basis we are already a middle-income economy with a per capita GDP hovering around $ 7,000. To add to that, India's traditionally high savings rate makes it a great place to invest in over at least a few decades.

Another increasingly good trend that India is seeing now is formalisation and financialisation of the economy. A favourite theme in a mid-income economy is the movement of market share from the informal sector to the formal sector. Demonetization (the Indian government de-notified high value notes of INR 500 and INR 1,000 in 2016 to curb the scourge of black money) and GST (goods and services tax, a form of value-added tax) have accelerated these trends. In industry after industry we are seeing that the larger organised players are getting market shares from unorganised players as their businesses become viable. Many of these businesses were flourishing by being able to evade direct and indirect taxes. In a value-added tax environment, they are unable to compete with more organised players who have economies of scale and a more efficient business model.

The biggest driver for formalisation is increasing brand and quality preference among consumers. Nowhere is the trend more visible than in the apparel and footwear space. Increasingly, consumer preference is clearly moving towards branded apparel segment. Page Industries has been one of the biggest success stories in the space. While the industry has been growing in low single digits, Page Industries has been showing a growth rate of over 27% over the last 11 years. Dollar Industries has grown over 17% in the same period. The mid-premium segment is growing at an even faster rate than the mid-segment and especially for low-value items, the brand preference is discernible. Relaxo Footwears, another player in the low-value branded segment of hawai slippers, has shown a CAGR in sales of over 20%, consolidating market share from unorganised and weaker players.

While the preference for brand in apparels is something one can see happening on a daily basis and is obvious, increasingly the same trend is visible in some of the industries earlier seen as a commodity play. Building materials space comprising sanitary ware, tiles, adhesives, electricals, laminates etc. is one such space. If one excludes sale by smaller players in the government housing schemes, broadly the market leaders in individual spaces like tiles, ply, cables, electrical, sanitary ware, paint etc have all consolidated their respective market share over the unorganised and smaller marginal players. For instance, Somany Ceramics, a leader in the tiling industry, has grown at a CAGR of over 16% in the last decade; Cera, a leading sanitary ware player, has grown at a CAGR of 24%; KEI, one of the leading electric cables manufacturer, has grown at over 15%; Asian Paints, industry leader in paints, has grown at over 15%. The growth for all these players has far outstripped the industry growth rate, as preference for brand and quality is becoming more discernible even in goods that are not necessarily meant for personal consumption.

The same trend is visible across multiple industries and a lot of hitherto price-sensitive segments are becoming more and more consumer-like with a clear preference for brand. We discussed basmati rice in the previous segment and how it is acquiring the colour of being a branded product instead of a commodity.

Spices, tyres, wheat flour which were sold as commodities a decade ago are now perceived as brands. As per capita income and population in middle-income group keep increasing, it is usual for more and more segments to be perceived as a brand. Industry leaders in such segments – moving from being commodities to brands – will continue to create tremendous value.

As one moves up the ladder of being a middle-income economy, the personal care segment typically also picks up. Multiple brands with different value propositions create a niche for themselves. New brands and new product propositions uproot some of the existing brands, but the willingness of the younger population to continue to spend more and more on personal care products keeps increasing. With so many different product lines and super-specialisations, there is often space for a newcomer to come up and create a name for oneself. Marico is one such example, which has grown virtually four-fold over the last decade or so. One single product, i.e Parachute hair oil, and brand extensions on hair-care segment still contribute to almost two-thirds of their sales. Other brands, like Lotus Herbals, CavinKare (Nyle), Medimix, Biotique and Fogg (Vini Cosmetics), too, have created strong brands that are reaching a threshold where they can become strong home-grown category leaders. While it is a difficult business to continuously scale up, surely some of them will give their international peers a run for their money.

With a younger population and increasing income levels, another macro trend becomes pronounced. A larger population starts to have access to credit and is willing to take more and more credit, not only for their businesses but also for consumer goods. The penetration of different forms of credit, like personal loan, credit cards, and loans for white goods, two-wheelers and education, keeps growing. This not only creates credit, but further fuels consumer demand and economy growth. The financial services industry will see strong players become stronger. While a lot of innovative models will continue to disrupt many businesses, the bigger players with access to cheaper funds will grow well as long as they can get their credit metrics right. One would think that over the next decade, larger private sector banks in India like HDFC, Kotak, ICICI and Axis will continue to become bigger and systemically more important. The Indian banking regulatory framework is reasonably strong and we have seen the regulator and the government crack the whip on private sector and public sector alike. This should keep the sector in good stead over a longer period of time.

Another sector that has been a laggard post-GFC but will continue to see a greater degree of formalisation and consolidation is real estate. Lately, we have seen that large conglomerates with strong pedigree like Mahindra, Tatas, Hero Group, Adani Group and Bharti Enterprises have all jumped on the real-estate bandwagon. Clearly, smart money is seeing an opportunity where unscrupulous players are vacating the space under their own debt burden, soft off-take and a stronger regulatory framework. It is hard to imagine that a country with increasing middle class and credit availability will not go back to consuming real estate with greater enthusiasm. As a new generation of consumers comes back, the rent yield goes up and the interest rates soften – this could be a sector which will see a lot of action in the 2020s. As an investor, one would do well to have a decent allocation in real estate space either directly or through stocks.

However, real estate is one sector that can easily become a reverse compounding machine if you take too much leverage or the company you are betting on has taken too much leverage. Like the credit business, where one would do well to back strong players with lower cost of capital, in real estate too one needs to back a player who is well-capitalised, has low cost of capital and a relatively well-diversified asset portfolio. A steady rental portfolio of commercial and retail assets gives tremendous staying power when the development business is going through a downturn. Needless to add, an understanding of micro-markets and demand-supply cycle is extremely important in this space.

There are states in the United States, like West Virginia, Illinois and Cleveland, which are seeing an absolute reduction in population. The population is aging too. It is hard to be betting on real-estate players over a decade in these markets. We talked about Japan earlier. It will require much more diligence and understanding of micro markets to be able to bet on real estate in these markets. In a younger India, with growing incomes and population, probably decision making is slightly easier as long as the hygiene factors are taken care of.

Another advantage of being a younger population is adoption of new technology and ability of the larger population to adjust to the changing skill-set requirements. India is already one of the largest per capital mobile data consumer in the world, consuming data at the rate of 11 gigabytes (GB) a month. This is incredible, given the differences in languages and large pockets of illiteracy. Even people in the lower echelons of the economic pyramid are not only able to use a mobile phone but are also able to consume large chunks of data for communication, entertainment and commerce.

This deep mobile penetration with access to good quality 4G data at an affordable price in itself is creating – and will create – hundreds of business models. For restaurants that only exist on a mobile phone, products only sold online, to payment gateways, yellow pages, matrimony sites, online classes, online credit, delivery of services etc. the potential for bridging the urban-rural divide over the next decade will be extraordinary. A large number of businesses will not be required to necessarily have most of their staff sitting out of their corporate office. Tier-II and tier-III towns will probably be able to stem some of its migration to cities with remote employment opportunities and access to quality healthcare and education happening on a remote basis.

Travel and tourism is another industry that has been blooming and will continue to bloom over the next couple of decades. However, the imprints of the sector dynamics and e-commerce are expected to play out extremely strongly in this space. Travel aggregators, OTA (online travel agents), ticketing platforms, meta search engines, hotel bookings, are all going to create millions of jobs and businesses. Players who cater to the right segment are going to create disproportionately more value. Players like Lemon Tree Hotels who operate in 3-star and 4-star segment and low-cost carriers like Indigo are rightly placed in segments that have an ever-increasing demand. India is still at the lower end of the mid-income economy class and the bulk of the demand will continue to be in the mid-income category services and products.

When an economy is in the low-income segment, a large portion of demand is for food, clothing and shelter. These businesses, and businesses ancillary to them, are where demand and growth outlook is positive. As economies enter the lower mid-income segment, the demand starts expanding to power, electricity and roads. The segments that cater to them see an exponential growth, and as one starts to cross the $ 10,000 PPP, that is when spend on healthcare, education and end-user services starts to grow at a much more rapid rate.

An interesting example in this space is the pressure cooker segment. Hawkins Cookers, one of the leaders in the pressure cooker segment, increased its sales from INR 187 crores to INR 653 crores in a span of 10 years without any additional capital raise and with large dividend payouts. The price of the stock went from INR 70 in 2007 to over INR 5,000 in 2020. The amount of wealth created for shareholders was huge. The same story with its competitor TTK Prestige, which increased its sales from INR 300 crores in 2008 to INR 2000 crores in 2020. The stock price went from about INR 100 to INR 7,000 per share. Each of these shares went 70 times over a period of 12 years and also consistently paid dividends to their shareholders.

Some of the white goods players, like Whirlpool, are creating a similar value for its shareholders. They have quadrupled their sales over the last decade or so, but their profits have increased by10 times and the share price by almost 100 times. If one can find quality management and strong brands in undiscovered spaces, the value accretion can be phenomenal. With increasing sales and brand value come increasing profitability, and as profitability expands faster than the sales, the multiples expand even faster. The key is to find these winners when they are still not on the radar of the institutional investors. With the income levels rising, the consumption of entry-level white goods is going to increase at a rapid rate. Pressure cookers and washing machines did well because demographically we have moved to a stage where people are willing to pay the price for automation to reduce their personal time consumed in daily chores.

As an investor who looks at these demographic trends, one needs to understand the exact status of where the economy is and identify some of these themes relatively early. It is not unusual to find market leaders of niche segments in a growing industry at an attractive valuation before they are 'discovered' by institutional investors. A market leader would more often than not have the ability to increase both pricing power and market share, and will increasingly start getting the multiples it deserves. The lesser the capex intensity and leverage, the sweeter the bargain.

PVR was a similarly undiscovered gem, with about a 100 screens and single digit multiples all the way up to 2011. A couple of years of IPL (Indian Premier League), a domestic T20 cricket league, had started to impact at least one quarter of their performance adversely, that too during the high-occupancy period of summer vacations. But as it started to get discovered institutionally, they consolidated market position, acquired smaller brands and became an undisputed leader in multiple major city centers in India. I like to call these market leaders in niche sub-billion dollar industries 'satraps'. Good satraps are rarely disturbed by Mr. Moneybags and have a better chance of winning over a challenger.

However, for this to play out, one needs to bet on an industry that we do not foresee to be disrupted at least in the foreseeable future. A very interesting example of how consumer behavior and technology impact businesses prone to disruption is Just Dial Ltd. The promoter of Just Dial, Mr. VSS Mani, had started a similar business called Ask Me in 1989; however, at that point India's tele-density was abysmal and mobile phones non-existent. Probably, it was an idea ahead of its time. In 1996, they launched again and had managed to get '88888 88888' as their universal dial-in. During the late-90s and early-2000s, mobile penetration in India was booming and call rates were coming down rapidly. In 2007 they started online web-based directories and mobile directories. It went from a INR 70 crores turnover to a INR 700 crores turnover from FY 2008 to FY 2017.

But suddenly some changes started happening in consumer behaviour. With the penetration of smartphones increasing, consumers started getting hooked on app-based services, and specialised apps started to cannibalise the yellow page business. There was a Zomato or a Swiggy, which had a much greater depth in the food business; there were travel aggregators like MakeMyTrip and Yatra, which meant that one did not need to speak to travel agencies; up came an Urban Clap, which helped with household handymen like carpenters, plumbers etc., and discount portals like Snapdeal (in its earlier avatar); Little and Nearbuy who started offering not only connects, but discounts for the neighbourhood salon, restaurant; Netmeds and 1mg will deliver medicines home; and players like IndiaMART started offering platforms that had full catalogues and price listings for B2B products. As the offerings of the specialists who did more than just listing grew richer, Just Dial has again started to see challenges with its growth. It is still relevant and will continue to be relevant but bit by bit a part of its business is being eaten by specialists. With a 5G auction on the way, the content and catalogue required for some of these platforms will further undergo change. Many instructive services, like teaching, healthcare, training programmes, conferences, will compel existing players to continue to enrich their product offering. It is best to be able to identify specialists who are least likely to be disrupted by such changes.

Even the biggest and the best are not immune

Every business gets impacted by the environment it operates in. One cannot, beyond a point, obsess over the environment to make investing decisions. But while finding stocks or sectors to back, it is important to have a perspective on future growth potential and rate of disruption in that industry. High-growth companies rightly get higher multiples and at times it may be worthwhile to pay more for quality. Most of the time companies in high-disruption industries also get very high multiples, which is a bit of a riskier proposition. To a multi-decade investor, a high rate of disruption is a red flag and not an enabler. Investors often assume that those who have been able to disrupt in the past will continue to be disruptors of the future, which may not always be true.

In 1990s and early 2000s, General Electric (GE) was seen as a gold-standard technology company. With business spanning from healthcare to aviation robotics and from financial services to renewable energy, it was a conglomerate that looked destined to keep growing. CEO Jack Welc htook the market capitalisation of GE from $ 12 billion in 1981 to $ 410 billion by the time he retired in 2001. Since then it has all been downhill and today GE is at $ 70 billion market capitalisation.

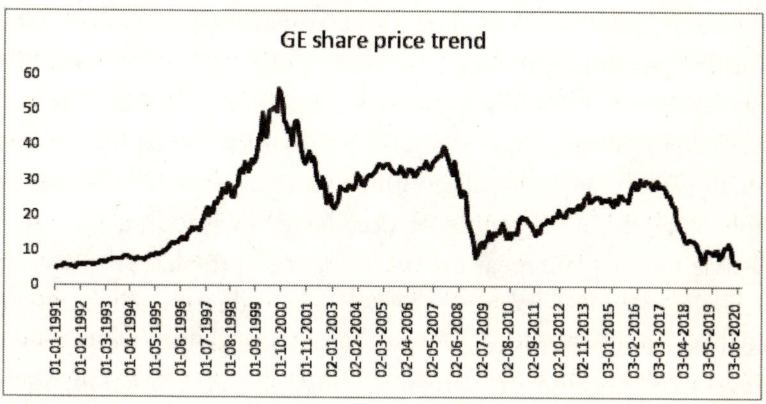

GE stock market price trend

It might sound very simple to park money with a giant who has shown an ability to grow even after becoming a giant, but one has to remember that leaders and managements have a finite life. Let us look at one of the most valuable companies in the world today, Apple, founded by Steve Jobs and Steve Wozniak. Due to differences with the board, Jobs resigned from the board in 1985, only to join back in 2007. The revenue growth there tells a story.

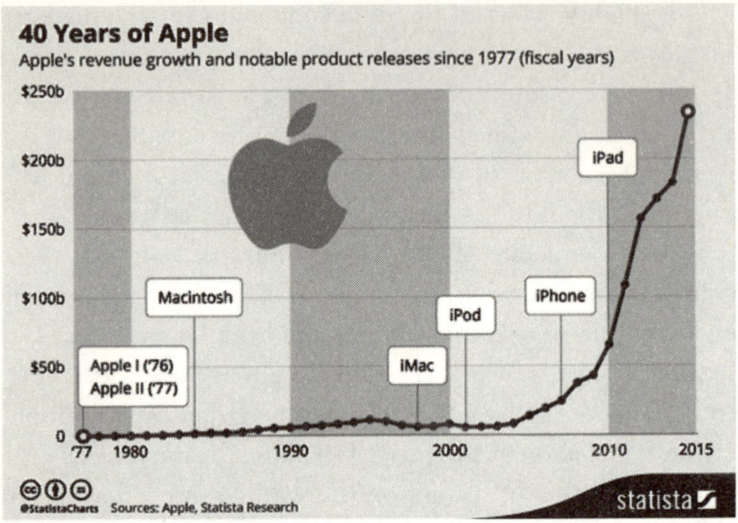

The re-induction of Jobs into the company led to new product launches, including the iconic iPod in 2001 and iPhone in 2007. The rest, as they say, is history. In 2020 it became a $2-trillion market capitalisation company. With Jobs not at the helm anymore, whether the company will continue to reinvent and maintain its mojo over the next couple of decades is anyone's guess, but to assume that it will repeat the performance of the last two decades is likely to be far-fetched. The telecom, tablets and computers business is inherently disruptive. One can already see existing players catching up on their core portfolio at a fraction of the price. Apple has been the disruptor over the last two decades under Jobs; we don't know where the next disruptor will come from.

If one has to look at emerging trends for the next couple of decades, one would do well to identify low middle-income and middle-income plays where consumers get better value for money. Better value for money can, however, not be equated with something cheap or inferior in quality or workmanship. One of the path-breaking products that was supposed to disrupt the automobile market was Tata Nano. One thought that India's price-sensitive population will queue up for the offering. Priced at INR 1,00,000, the car was supposed to be significantly cheaper than any other four-wheeler in the space. The closest rival at that time, Maruti 800, was priced more than twice that – but the product did not click. In fact, over the next decade, Maruti, actually, phased out its flagship Maruti 800 from the market as there was a discernible consumer shift from small cars to the compact sedan market (sedans of less than four-meter length).

Bajaj, which was traditionally known for its scooter business and was an omnipresent brand and identified with scooters, phased out their scooter business around 2013. They could sense a shift of consumer preference from scooters to motorcycles as income levels were improving. It is a different matter that growth in scooters made a comeback, targeting a new segment of teenagers and women, riding on the theme of 'easy to ride'. The new demand in scooters was not driven by the cost argument and they were never meant to be cheaper alternatives to the motorcycle. An understanding of some of the finer nuances of the demographic shifts can be an extremely useful tool in the arsenal of an investor.

Demographic themes for the next few decades

A very important aspect of a mid-income economy adding to its GDP is the progressively lower cost of capital. The country's credit rating (irrespective of what the rating agencies may say) starts improving in the eyes of the providers of capital. More data and history are available to be able to price credit rightly, and most decent size companies have access to equity capital to correct their balance sheets in adverse times. The regulatory framework with regards to recovery starts getting crystallised and bankruptcy laws get streamlined.

The lowering cost of capital for a country as a whole accelerates the infrastructure development process for the country and has a multiplier effect on the economy. Although infrastructure creators need and get large pools of capital, there are other ancillary businesses that are less in capex intensity and show better returns on equity. Players in the EPC space, electrical equipment players, railway wagon manufacturers and engineering companies are the ones who may end up creating a larger value from a shareholder's perspective as they have relatively better insulation from market cycles and, at the same time, don't need to keep raising large pools of external capital to grow.

Let us look at IRB Infrastructure, a large road EPC player with a decent pool of BOT assets, which saw its construction sales increase from INR 567 crores to INR 5,410 crores from FY 2009 to FY 2019. The company managed to churn seven of its toll assets into an InvIT[3] (infrastructure investment trust) structure in May 2017, giving them access to a low-yield, low-risk capital, and in the process making itself asset-light and reducing leverage.

This also enabled it to bid more aggressively for further road projects. In 2020, they struck a deal with GIC to create another private InvIT to further deleverage their balance sheet. Access to such cheap sources of capital for the infrastructure industry takes away many other risks from the business. As the InvIT and the REIT (real estate investment trust) market in India matures further, the ability of some of these players to deploy large pools of capital in their core development business will create huge value and de-risk businesses. One will do well to keep an eye on this segment and as

3. InvIT is a structure where a revenue-generating infrastructure asset is parceled out to yield investors. With development risks behind it, the perceived risk is lower, bringing down cost of capital for the infrastructure player.

the depth in yield plays for India increases, ancillary industries will keep growing in size and create even more value.

IndiGrid, a transmission company, managed to do the same for its transmission assets, in the process not only deleveraging their balance sheet, but also improving the parent's credit-rating and reducing their cost of debt.

Another sector that is going to benefit from the demographics is the contract manufacturing space. The ones catering to the consumer sector, like Dixon Technologies, which does consumer durables, lighting and mobile phones. and Amber Enterprises, which makes air conditioners, will continue to find more and more business. The fact that they cater to multiple brands de-risks their business significantly. It is not a surprise that these players get very attractive multiples from the market. However, there are other players in the contract manufacturing or quasi-contract manufacturing space that may grow equally well but do not attract a similar kind of attention. Most auto-component players are, in a way, contract manufacturers for their OEMs but do not enjoy even half the multiples that Amber and Dixon enjoy. Some of the well diversified plays that don't get disrupted by new technologies will create value. Contract manufactures for the pharma sector and the agro-chemical space will also grow. However, these are fragmented businesses and identifying players who have access to regulated markets and have a diversified client base will grow faster.

India also is rapidly becoming an insured country. Under the Pradhan Mantri Jan Arogya Yojna (PMJAY), almost 10.74 crore families and 50 crore individuals are being provided a healthcare coverage. Similarly, under the central government's crop insurance plan, a large number of marginal farmers are getting covered. Insuring the weaker sections of society will have a transformational impact on their lives over a longer period of time. So many citizens from the marginalised sections of society keep falling back into the poverty trap due to illness in the family or crop failures. Insurance will ensure a sustained level of consumption and financial security for those who need it the most, and hopefully improve their lives significantly over the next decade.

Themes that cater to the emerging middle class will also play strong over the next few years. Indian multi-brand retail has been a graveyard for various players, whether it was on the agri-retail space, mobile retail or conventional retail. Advent of e-commerce, restrictions on FDI and high rentals have all made this business challenging to say the least. Amidst all this mayhem, there was one retailing format that has not been badly impacted by the above factors and has carved a niche is the value retail segment serving the emerging middle class.

V-Mart, the market leader in the value retail segment, saw its sales move from INR 98 crores in FY 2008 to INR 1,434 crores in 2019. The profit went from INR 4 crores to INR 62 crores. Being an early leader in a space that catered to the right demography not impacted by the high rental costs in cities helped it create efficiencies of scale and also create a brand. A low-margin business with a huge network effect makes it difficult for new players to compete as well in the space. Geographical diversity in tastes and preferences allows the format to have multiple players while flying below the radar of larger competitors in the retail space.

The same story holds true for Jubilant FoodWorks, which is the master franchisee for Domino's Pizza in India. The restaurant industry has also been a very tricky industry to say the least and very few players have managed to survive the high rentals, changing tastes and challenges from new formats. Jubilant FoodWorks, armed with a global brand like Domino's, created a model that was light on real estate and a business model with a relatively lean menu. Add to that a demography of the young, which was consuming American sitcoms, travelling more often and starting to live in a nuclear family. They cracked a sweet niche by promising to deliver within 30 minutes of the order being placed, which Indian food players could not offer because of the sheer variety and preparation time. The cocktail worked like magic. The sale of Jubilant went from INR 424 crores in FY 2010 to INR 3,563 crores in FY 2019. Profits went almost 10x and the stock price went almost 12x over the period. If one can identify these satraps that cater to the right demography early on, they can make a marked difference to portfolio performance. Probably it is only fair to say that the Indian stock market, which may look like a treacherous coal mine, is abundantly littered with diamonds like these too.

7

Currency Cycle

The journey of investing across cycles is a most enriching one as it gives multiple tools in the hands of the investors to evaluate businesses, business environment, and to price their bet accordingly. All the other cycles we discussed earlier typically help make money across their curves. However, the trickiest of them all is the currency cycle. A rapidly depreciating currency will destroy value almost across all asset classes with a possible exception of maybe gold.

When currencies for very large economies are under pressure, we see a flight of capital to what are deemed safe haven currencies or assets. Traditionally, over centuries gold has been seen as a safe haven asset and whenever there is a run on the currency, there is a tendency to hoard gold. Over the last half a century or so, US government securities have also been seen as a store of value and an asset class one would go to when looking for a safe haven asset.

Countries worldwide started holding larger and larger pools of their assets in the form of US dollar, giving it a status of reserve currency in the world. The fact that most of the global trade was also happening in US dollar or linked to dollar values further strengthened the status of dollar.

Risks of expansionary fiscal and monetary policies

To give the world an alternate reserve currency, which is backed by a comparable sized economy, members of the European Union got together on 1st January 1999 to create a new currency called 'euro'. Most of the major economies in Europe, spanning 19 countries, including Germany, France, Italy, Netherlands and Greece, decided to move to the euro as their only currency. However, the British while being part of the European Union (which they later exited in January 2020) did not choose to adopt the euro as their currency. Similarly, the Swiss and the Danish continued with their own respective currencies, which did take away from the stature of the euro somewhat as an alternative to the US dollar.

Later, expansionary fiscal policies of some of the member countries like Ireland, Greece, Spain and Portugal meant that the European Union had to give bailouts to these countries from time to time post-GFC. This has somewhat increased the fragility in the Eurozone. The stronger economies feel that they are having to bail out the weaker ones, and the weaker ones feel constrained by not being allowed to undertake independent fiscal and monetary policy measures. For instance, Greece was the largest recipient of the bailout package and was forced to take deep cuts in its public spending programmes. Politically, these cuts were extremely unpopular and led to a lot of political uncertainty and churn in Greece during those times.

In the absence of the levers of liberal fiscal and monetary policies, the GDP of Greece came down from $ 354 billion in 2010 to $ 195 billion in 2016 before it started to recover again. While the forced cuts have brought a semblance of discipline back in the Greek economy, such a rapid decline in economy has prohibitive human costs in terms of income levels, unemployment and standards of livings in general.

In the previous chapter we discussed how a few countries, which do not have a well-functioning democracy, used a very liberal monetary policy regime, trying to print their way out of economic slowdowns. Invariably, when one starts to disrespect own currency, disaster waits. Nothing has been more catastrophic than Venezuela – an economy that till early 2010s was growing rapidly and was seen as a relatively stable economy, thanks to its oil reserves. Then the fiscal deficit numbers started to shoot up in 2011, and consistently stayed in double digits from 2012 onwards. The currency started losing value and the impact on GDP was unimaginable.

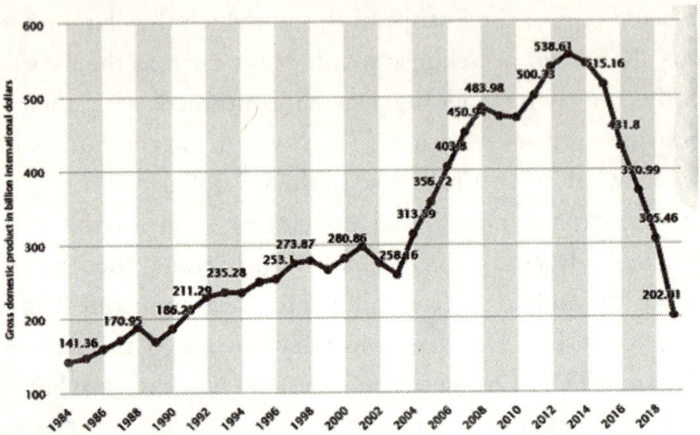

Source: Statista

The impact of such a steep and rapid fall in GDP was unbelievably heartrending. By 2017, according to *Time* magazine, the average Venezuelan lost 11 kg of weight in the year 2017 and approximately 90 percent of the population are not able to purchase enough food on a daily basis. Reuters reported that a UN report estimated in March 2019 that 94% of Venezuelans live in poverty, and more than 10% of Venezuelans (3.4 million) left their country. The UN analysis estimates in 2019 suggested that 25 percent of Venezuelans need some form of humanitarian assistance. Venezuela led the world in murder rates, with 81.4 per 100,000 people killed in 2018, making it the third most violent country in the world.

There are many poor countries where basic human needs are difficult to meet, but to have a lot and lose a lot of it in a relatively short span of time creates unrest and despondency, which make the countries unstable. Both Greece and Venezuela were doing alright in the first decade of the millennium, but within the span of a decade they have seen a lot. While Greece took corrective steps in terms of public spending and is getting back on its feet, Venezuela seems to be continuing its journey into the black hole.

Economies that have a very liberal deficit financing and monetary policy do invariably end up with high inflation and pressure on their respective currencies. In the initial period this higher deficit financing can stimulate the economy and lead to more consumption and better profits for some of the corporates. But if the same is done on a sustained basis, it starts to erode the purchasing power and value of the savings of the population, creating a negative wealth effect and pushing the economy into a downward spiral. Most mature economies, therefore, keep an eagle eye on the stability of their currency.

As an investor who is looking to invest in multiple countries will do well to be extremely conscious of currency risk. No matter what your skills in terms of stock picking and investing are, if the currency in question depreciates rapidly, you have very little chance of making money in that geography. A rapid currency depreciation is rarely an isolated event; it brings with it deterioration in earnings capability, future investments and a government's future investment capabilities. Not only that, it starts to scare foreign investment and can also encourage the wealthier population of those countries to migrate, further worsening the situation. In an extreme situation like Venezuela, civil unrest and worsening of law and order follow.

For most students of economics, a liberal monetary policy would equate to higher inflation and higher interest rates; still a large part of the developed world has been able to sustain low interest rates and liberal fiscal policies for over a decade now. We are now increasingly entering a territory where countries are able to raise extremely long-tenor debt like a 100-year bond or a perpetual bond at very little cost. For instance, Austria managed to raise a 100-year bond in mid-2019 at an annual yield of 1.17%.

At the time of the issue, Germany's 10-year bond had a yield of a negative 0.32%. Even Japan had a negative yield on a 10-year paper. The desperation for yield on secure assets is pushing investors to the longer end of the curve. This is bringing down yields on longer tenor instruments too.

We are increasingly seeing stronger economies across the world use liberal monetary policies, like lower interest rate and liquidity creation in the time of slowdown to regain their export competitiveness and to stimulate the economy back to growth. Many major economies in early 2020 had a government debt to GDP ratio in excess of 100%, along with very low interest rates. In fact, G-Sec yields of many high-income First World stable economies were below 1%.

There is an enormous amount of liquidity in the world, which is chasing small returns in exchange of security. Countries that can demonstrate fiscal and monetary discipline will probably be able to access more and more capital at a cheaper rate. One would love to be an equity investor in countries where one can raise such a low cost of capital on a sustainable basis. Long-tenor cheap debt can bump up your equity returns significantly.

However, while some of the countries are able to do it because of the strengths of their economy, the case of the US is unique. The US is able to consistently print its way out of recession, partly because of its status as the reserve currency of the world. In the wake of the Covid crisis, the US has taken an extremely large expansionary plan, which has swelled the balance sheet of the Federal Reserve System; the Committee for a Responsible Federal Budget estimated that the budget deficit for fiscal year 2020 could be a record \$ 3.8 trillion or 18.7% of the country's GDP. This is on the back of a \$ 984 billion deficit in the year 2019, which was 4.7% of the GDP. Just to give a sense, only four countries – the US, China, Japan and Germany – have a GDP that exceeds \$ 3.8 trillion. Let's look at the chart on the Fed's balance sheet, which is drilling holes through the ceiling:

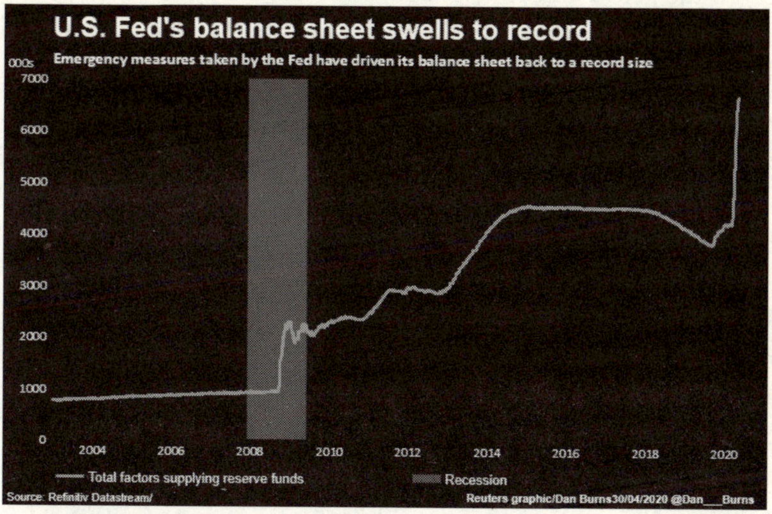

Source: stousifled.org

The Fed's balance sheet in May 2020 spiked to $ 6.8 trillion, which is almost equal to a third of the US GDP. While the status of reserve currency does provide some protection, it is going to be a Herculean task to unwind such positions. With China sitting on over $3 trillion of forex reserves and being increasingly seen as an adversary, the risk to dollar hegemony is getting accentuated. It is, thus, not a surprise that the traditional safe haven of gold is seeing a golden run in its prices.

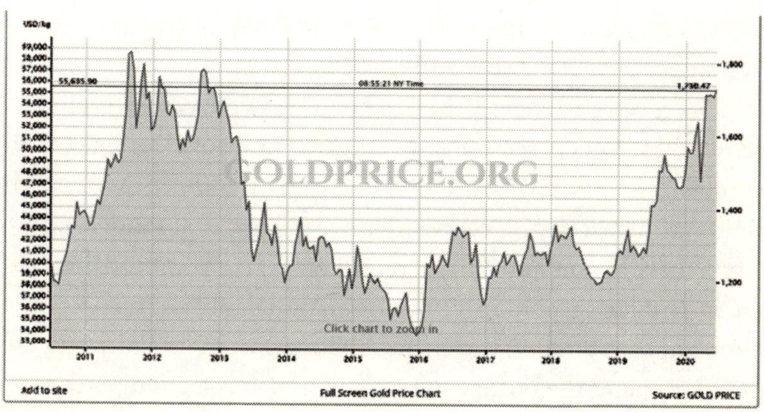

Given the geo-political dynamics involved, it is difficult to predict how the cookie will crumble and how the Fed will be able to downsize its balance sheet and how long the US dollar's unbridled hegemony will last – but clearly it is facing its toughest test in at least the last 50 years.

While a lot of this is something an investor can do very little about, and if at all there is pressure on the US dollar, it is not only the US that will be impacted; countries with a large pool of their assets in US-denominated securities will also be scarred.

The strength of the US currency has got to do as much with the country's geo-political strength as it has got to do with the size of its economy. Even with such high deficits, it will take a brave man to bet against their currency due to the sheer size of their economy and some of their corporations having operations across the world. One would think that they will find a way to gradually inflate out the debt while keeping the interest rates low rather than experiencing a currency shock.

Some currencies have higher intrinsic value than their traded value

How can an investor benefit from the understanding of currencies? The way to look at it would be that even someone who is primarily an equity investor will do well to diversify their asset allocation, both in terms of geography and in terms of asset classes. This becomes even more important if you are living in a country which has an expansionary fiscal and monetary policy.

However, currency cycles are not always adverse. Devaluation and currency depreciation do create immense value of the manufacturing companies and create export competitiveness. The trick is to invest in the economy after a big devaluation and not before that. If you can find a reasonably functioning democracy that is willing to abide by its international obligations to other nations and multilateral agencies like the International Monetary Fund (IMF) and the European Commission, it is a good place to go.

Let's look at Thailand, and what happened to Thailand after the Asian financial crisis of 1997. From 1985 to 1996, the Thai baht was pegged to the US dollar at 25 THB (Thai bahts). Following the East Asian crisis, the Thai baht came under serious pressure through speculative attacks and eventually the government was forced to float it in 1997. The THB lost more than half the value and started trading at 56 THBs for a US dollar by January 1998, before starting to gradually find its way back.

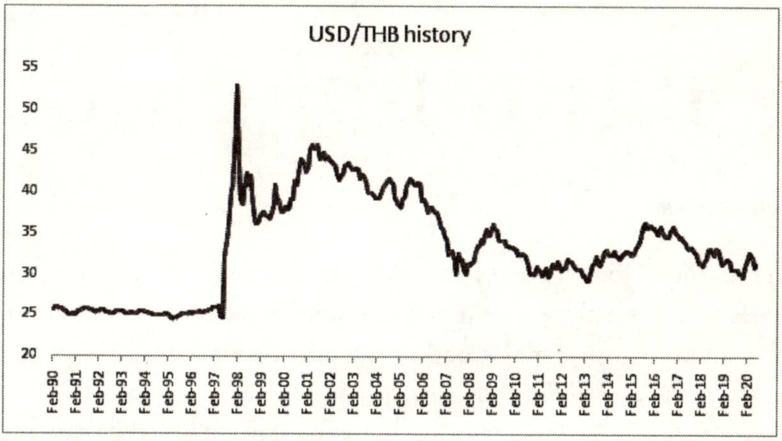

Source: Investing.com

What helped Thailand was a relatively more open economy with a cheaper currency, making it an attractive export destination; the cost of labour and other material became cheaper compared to the rest of the world. In late 1990s it almost felt like the heavens had fallen, and in many ways it had fallen too. But if someone invested in the Thai Index fund SET50 (Thailand's benchmark index) in 1998, after it went to free float, he would have made 5x-6x returns in THBs. As one can see, the currency also appreciated from its low of 56 to close to 30 THBs to a dollar. Dollar returns would have been north of 10x, not a bad 22-year dollar return for index investing. However, a similar bet on a country that refuses to get its fiscal discipline corrected could make you a pauper very fast.

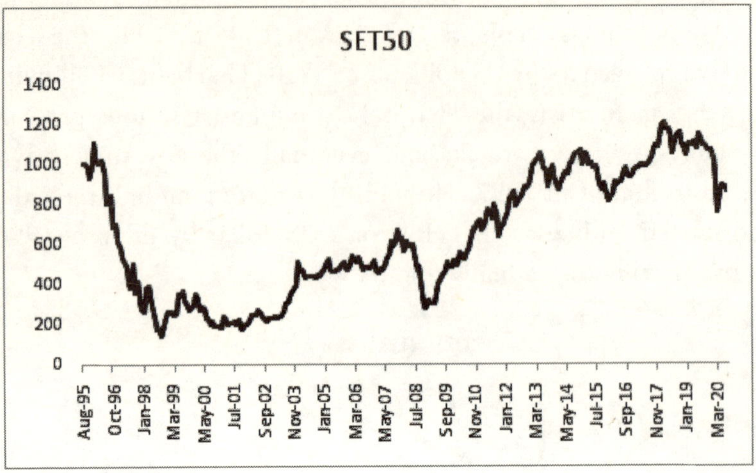

Source:set.or.th

Let us now look at another example from the Asian financial crisis to demonstrate that this was not an isolated case. Let's look instead at the other major and independent economy at the center of the same crisis –South Korea.

South Korea had a very similar experience when they saw the won (South Korean currency) collapse from less than 800 won/dollar to 1700 won/dollar in 1998.

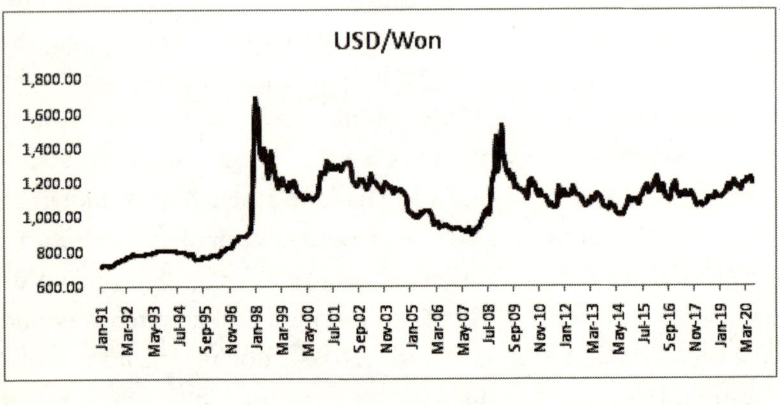

Source:investing.com

However, the economy soon started to find its mojo back and the KOSPI (the Korea Composite Stock Price Index) has given a 5x index return since then and at the same time, the currency has appreciated back to 1200 wons to a dollar.

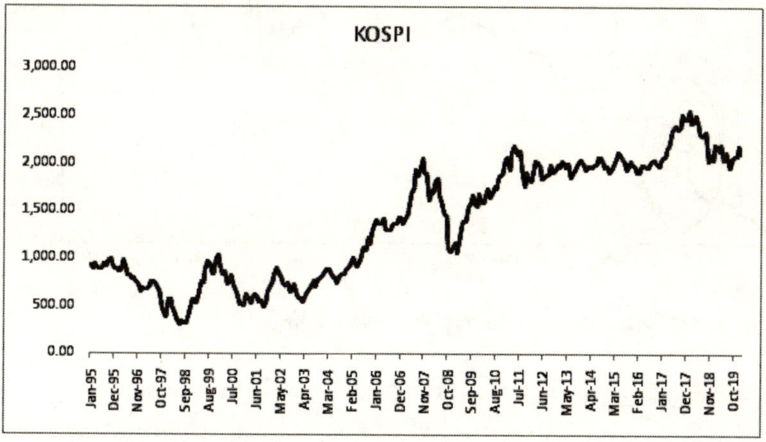

Source: investing.com, KOSPI performance

So, if one gets into sweet economies when they have had an adverse market cycle and an adverse currency cycle, there will be money made going forward if the country maintains its fiscal rectitude. What is important while playing the currency cycle is to be acutely aware of the red flags, which might make the country a slippery slope to an abyss like a Venezuela or a Zimbabwe. Democracy, fiscal rectitude and willingness to abide by global commitments area *sine qua non* for investing in these geographies.

Managing currency risks in emerging economies

India has had its own flirtations with the vexatious currency cycles, and invariably post-devaluation investments have brought mid-term prosperity for stock market investors. The two cycles of devaluation that distinctly come to mind are the ones during the 1991 crisis and the rapid depreciation that happened between 2010 and 2013.

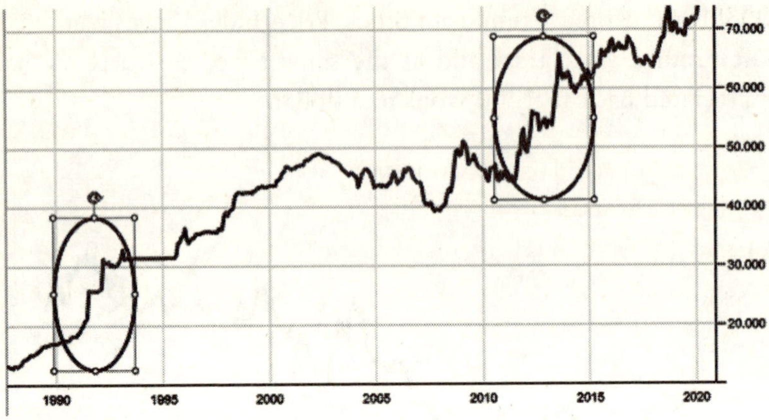

Source: tradingeconomics.com, USD/INR graph

These are the two periods in the past three decades when the Indian currency depreciated relatively fast in a relatively short span of time. Both these periods were followed by liberalisation and fiscal rectitude to get the government finances in order. However, the Indian currency did continue to have a secular depreciating trend vis-à-vis the US dollar but the stock market returns were stratospheric. While the currency depreciated from 30 to 45 between 1995 and 2011, the stock exchange went from 3000 to 20,000, a 4-5x dollar return over 15 years. Similarly, post-2013, while the currency depreciated at a relatively mild rate, the stocks exchange went from 20,000 to 40,000 from 2013 to 2019. As an investor who is looking to allocate money across multiple geographies, some of these currency trends and the government's commitments towards fiscal responsibility are an extremely important barometer of capital allocation.

Let us look at each of these periods individually. In 1991, India had its worst foreign exchange crisis and was on the verge of sovereign default. The country had to airlift its gold reserves to get a bailout from the IMF. In order to get its export competitiveness back, India had to devalue its currency by 20% in July 1991 and make structural reforms to open up the economy. At that point of time, there was very stringent opposition to the step but it paid rich dividends for the country as a whole, improving the quality of living and spurring GDP growth in real earnest. This was one of the watershed events in India's economic history which could in some ways be compared to the Thai devaluation.

The depreciation in Indian currency in 2011 and 2014 was spurred by high budgetary deficit financing by the government to support social sector schemes. This led to the inflation rate to shoot back above the 10% mark. This was coupled with widespread allegations of corruption and crony capitalism, leading to a policy paralysis within the government. The currency depreciated from INR 45 to a dollar to INR 66 to a dollar in virtually no time. A rapid depreciation along with crony capitalism led to despondency among the investor community. This was a precipice from where India could have potentially gone down either the path of further expansionary monetary and fiscal policy or towards fiscal consolidation. Thankfully, the country chose the latter and, in hindsight, that made all the difference. The currency only depreciated marginally, and the benchmark stock indices virtually became two and a half times.

Brazil was in a similar situation in 2016 and, in roughly three years, the currency depreciated to half its value. Where in 2013 the Brazilian real was trading at 2 reals for a dollar, it moved to 4 reals for a dollar in 2016. The fiscal deficit was at a staggering 10.2% in 2015 and one felt that a lot could go wrong for the economy.

Brazil took a slightly soft-landing kind of an approach and brought down its fiscal deficit from 10.2% to 5.9% by 2019, while progressively committing to continuing to eliminate its primary deficit. Because of the soft-landing approach, the economy did not crash, but has been in a sub 1% growth rate over the last five years. They have also allowed the currency to float and depreciate a bit more over the last three years. The Brazilian stock index responded beautifully to the fiscal responsibility measures being taken and the Ibovespa went from

40,000 in 2016 to 1,20,000 by end of 2019. One does get a feeling that with a further depreciation of currency in early 2020, the government is probably back in a position to loosen its belt and look at the next cycle of growth.

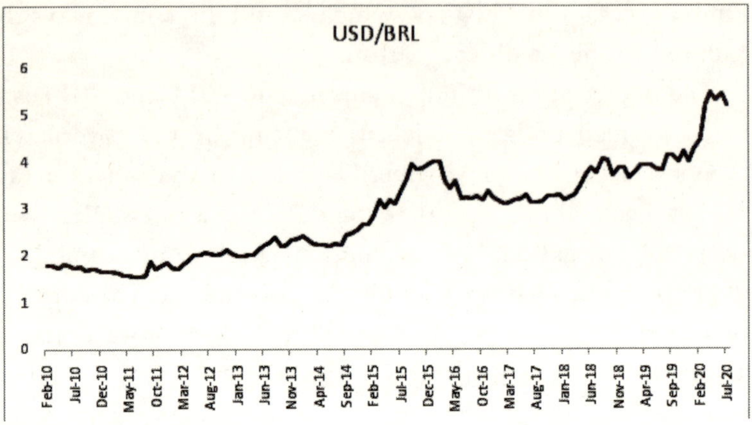

Source:Investing.com

Large stable economies with strong institutions have their own way to find a balance after excesses. Even if there are periods of inertia and poor fiscal discipline, the institutions force you to course-correct and do the right thing over a longer period of time. Stability and trust in a currency are hallmarks of trust in the sustainability of the economy itself. Global capital does find its way into geographies that keep their house in order and protect their currencies from dramatic moves.

An emerging economy like India or Brazil do need all pools of foreign capital to achieve their growth objectives, to be able to build infrastructure of tomorrow and to provide healthcare and education access to their large populations. Like a person who spends more than he earns for his daily consumption expenses, and struggles to pay his monthly bills, gets his credit rating downgraded, leading to an increase in interest rate, larger outstanding balances leading to a higher cost of capital and reduced paying capability. This is what we call a debt trap. The same is true for nations. Thankfully, nations have more means, more resources and more levers to manage their balance sheet unlike individuals. One does feel that both India and Brazil are doing reasonably well in their ability to contain fiscal deficits and will see extended periods of relative stability in currency and lowering cost of capital for their respective governments and economies.

Most global funds do study the currency cycle very closely from a capital allocation perspective. But a study of currency cycle and its impact has applications for a single country investor also. For instance, if you are in a rapidly depreciating currency with limited fiscal discipline, you would want to allocate part of your assets in gold or foreign assets like the US government securities. If you believe that a country is looking to depreciate its currency gradually to stay competitive for exports, you should look at opportunities in the export domain, where the country has competencies.

One of the prime example of such a policy is Bangladesh, which through a calibrated depreciation and focus on exports, has become the second largest exporter of ready-made garments in the world. The ready-made garments sector grew at the rate of a whopping 55%[4] year on year between 2002 and 2012.

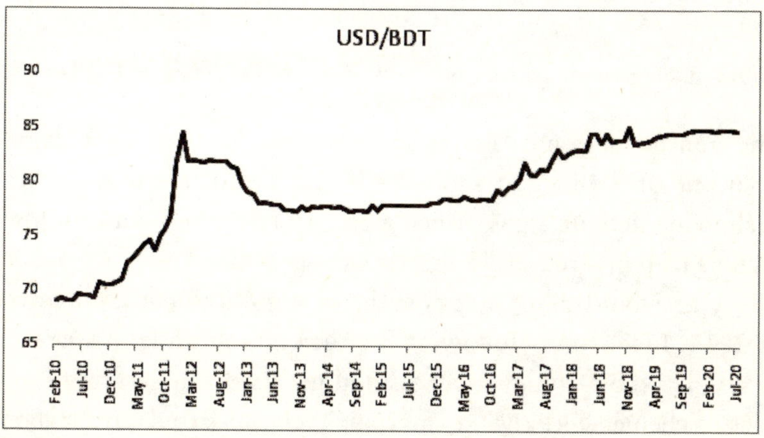

Source:investing.com

4. (Source: Uddin M. How the Bangladeshi ready-made garment industry can be competitive in the global market. Business Economics and Tourism. 2014:1–68.)

A moderate depreciation from 68 Bangladeshi takas to 84 takas to a dollar from 2008 to 2012 allowed Bangladesh to continue to stay export-competitive, while other Asian countries were losing their exports to China. Cheaper labour and favourable government policies also helped in this phenomenal transformation for one of the poorest countries in the world in terms of per capita income. This is also the country which came into existence only in 1971 and at the time of their independence had one of the worst HDI (Human Development Index) in the world.

Bangladesh per capita GDP in USD

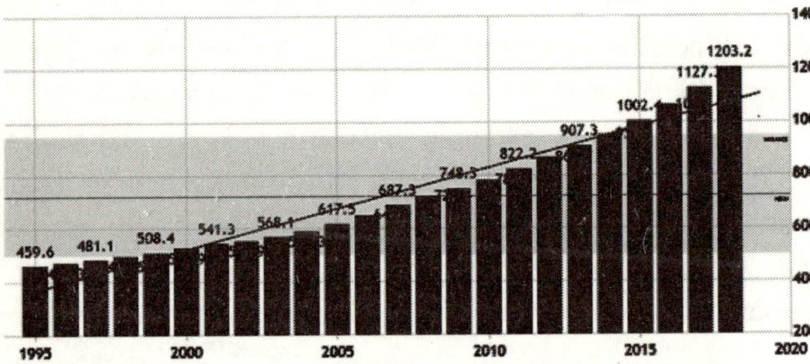

Source: tradingeconomics.co, worldbank, Bangladesh Per Capita GDP in USD

The transformation of Bangladesh over the last two decades has been one of the biggest successes in the world, where a country is showing definite signs of being able to take itself out of a low-income trap in a relatively shorter time period.

One would think that post the new government taking over in 2014, India too is following a policy of soft glide in currency to retain export-competitiveness and get its manufacturing mojo back. Schemes like 'Make in India', cluster-based government policies, a hawkish focus on managing fiscal deficit and a reducing corporate tax rate are all a part of the larger game-plan to make India an important and globally competitive manufacturing hub. This is important not only from the perspective of shoring up forex reserves but also to provide employment opportunities to India's teeming millions, as an ever larger number of people keep joining the workforce every day.

For a larger and slightly more prosperous economy like India, the sectors to flourish might be in the more value-added segment. One would believe that apart from traditional sectors like textile and gems and jewelry, India will continuously be able to shore up its manufacturing base in engineering goods, electronics, telecom equipment, pharma, specialty chemicals, auto and auto-components in general and electric vehicles value chain specifically as they move along. Services export on IT and ITeS (information technology enabled services) is something India has done traditionally well in, and one would hope this will expand to a lot more fields like media content, digital services, travel aggregation, robotics, artificial intelligence etc. over the next few years. As an investor, one would do well to look at some of the sector leaders in the space as they emerge, especially those looking at exports markets to back. However, one needs to continue to be cautious of taking bets in sectors that have a very large upfront capex and is seeing large investor appetite. Most such businesses gradually end up selling their wares on a marginal cost basis, seriously impacting the return of capital and equity returns for the business.

Another very interesting way to look at investing in geographies which are continuously but gradually depreciating their currencies is that they are building a store of value. This might be counter-intuitive at first, as one would think that a depreciating currency erodes value. However, if a depreciating currency creates export competitiveness and brings economic growth and builds forex reserves, gradually the intrinsic value of the currency becomes much stronger than what it trades at. Theoretically, one would expect a currency depreciation to be linked to the inflation rate in the economy. A country with a higher inflation rate will depreciate at a rate higher than a country with a lower inflation rate.

In some cases the difference in relative depreciation can

be lower than the theoretical depreciation rate on a sustained basis if the currency has a fair value higher than its traded rate. Gradually, the discrepancy between the fair value of the currency and its traded value becomes large enough to force the economy to course-correct and revalue the currency upwards. China did it very successfully over the first decade of the millennium. They had pegged their currency to the US dollar and you got 8.27 RMBs to a dollar. The rate was pegged at a level that made Chinese exports to the world extremely competitive, making it the manufacturing powerhouse of the world. Over the years the export competitiveness reached a level where there was global pressure on China to revalue its currency upwards to correct the global balance of trade mismatches. Again in 2008, during the GFC, China reverted to the dollar peg at 6.83 yuan to a dollar and, when the float was removed again in 2010, the yuan appreciated to almost 6 RMBs to a dollar. China's float in the market is what economists call a dirty float, where the government and the central bank play a very active role in ensuring that currency movements are managed not only for volatility but also for their absolute levels and general direction.

We have seen how rapid devaluation in the Thai baht helped it get its manufacturing mojo back and subsequent consistent appreciation in currency. One would think the approach towards a currency is also largely determined by which stage of the evolution of an economy one is in. A low-income or a low mid-income economy, which is looking to spur its economy through export competitiveness, will always prefer a softer gliding currency regime. As the economy grows and one becomes a high mid-income economy, the dynamics change. Manufacturing is not the biggest gun in the arsenal and the economy starts getting driven more towards services and consumption. At that point, having a sliding cheaper currency may become undesirable and make one's imports expensive. Also, the products you are selling are not as price sensitive as some of the commodities a poorer economy sells, hence your ability to sell those products and services are not determined by price alone.

An understanding of demographics, income levels and currency movements in a country are often intertwined, and the discourse on one is not complete without the other. The movements in these have an extremely strong bearing on public policy and the direction a country takes. And this is also what makes me extremely optimistic about India as a country. The country is at that sweet spot where it is moving from a low mid-income economy to a mid-income economy; the rising forex reserves coupled with a moderately depreciating currency is creating a store of value, and we have been extremely focused as a country on our commitment to fiscal responsibility.

8

Sunrise Industries – Snowballs and Raita

While we have covered part of how sunrise industries play out in product life cycles, this is one aspect that probably gets a lot of interest from investors and students of investing. This is how to play the sunrise industry, which is attracting mammoth investor interest and is, in the process, creating a whole new industry. Probably the phenomenon has been around for at least a century and a half, if not more, when the British railroads were being built and everyone wanted a share in the railroad companies. But with the rate of disruption in the world increasing and cost of capital coming down, these cycles have become more frequent and have started to have a life of their own.

These are explosive cycles, where initially the cost is high and returns are lower, but increasingly more and more industry participants, as well as investors, start getting more and more excited about the opportunity, pushing the technology curve ahead, bringing down per unit costs and creating an even bigger market, which progressively further brings down the cost, creates more customers and gets even more investor interest. This is the classic 'snowball' effect, which keeps making the ball bigger as it rolls, the operating leverage of the slope adding velocity and the environment adding mass.

These are transformational cycles, because they not only create a new industry, but often take mankind forward. However, as an investor, it does not mean that it is easy to make money in a sunrise industry. As a student of investing, one needs to carefully understand who has the bargaining power in the entire build-out and who can afford to play his cards late. Often, investors who play the game late benefit a lot more than early movers. The early movers do all the hard work of bringing down costs, build an eco-system, educate the customer and get customer acceptance, and the late movers swoop in with lesser capital outlay and efficient execution. But the consumer surplus it creates changes the industry and often the world for good.

Like the UK railroads experience in the middle of the 19th century, where a liberal licensing policy for building out railroads created a virtual mania and both investors and entrepreneurs alike were queuing up to get in. Many competing railroads were laid between same destinations, compromising on their commercial viability. Eventually, much money was lost by investors, but England became dramatically better off, with a superb railway network.

The solar power sector went through a similar experience, where large pools of capital chasing the sector kept bringing down the price of solar power rapidly and creating graveyards of companies across the value chain of solar manufacturing. But this also accelerated the adoption of cleaner solar power at a competitive price.

We discussed the LED light business briefly and how some of the older players managed to transition smoothly into that space. But the industry itself went through a similar pain. In India, scores of entrepreneurs got into the business of making LED lights and innovative models like zero-capital cost and power-saving sharing etc. started to evolve.

In the middle of this, India's public sector ESCO (energy service company), Energy Efficiency Services Ltd. (EESL), got into a rapid

LED light buying spree. The intent was to help every household have LED lights to bring down India's power consumption and to get municipalities to use power-efficient LED lights instead of halogen bulbs. The scheme had the direct backing of the prime minister, Narendra Modi. Street lights and public lighting spaces also started getting replaced at a rapid rate, with the existing halogen lights being replaced by LED lights. This created a huge demand for LED lights in the country, and with China willing to supply LED chips, the assembly was not very capital intensive.

New players who wanted to capture market share started to bid extremely aggressively and often at marginal cost, with the hope that volumes would bring efficiency to production. According to ELCOMA (Electric Light and Component Manufacturers' Association), the LED market grew at the rate of a whopping 74% between 2012 and 2016. Under the central government procurement plan, the price of a LED bulb fell from INR 310 per bulb in January 2014 to INR 38 by September 2016. The business model became unsustainable. Even strong incumbents were facing huge headwind and the loss of market share was hurting. The smarter ones decided to cede market share and concentrate on their distribution channels and other products, and started to withdraw from EESL bids. Many players in the space who had got private equity funding and hired star brand ambassadors, went bankrupt or incurred heavy losses.

The entire excitement around the product not only created the industry but made it well entrenched in less than half a decade. Power savings for the country as a whole was phenomenal. As of the end of financial year 2019, according to an estimate under the government's LED bulb distribution programme, more than 25 crore bulbs were distributed, leading to an estimated power saving of 6,725 MW of peak demand. *(Source: The Economic Times)*

Digital disruption

The digital world on the aggregation side is going through a similar funding cycle. It is unfair to club them together as one industry, as each business model is unique and looking to cater to diverse needs and a diverse customer base. However, what is common to previous themes is that it is encouraging entrepreneurs to create more and more digital businesses, and these digital businesses are creating huge consumer surpluses[5] and offering newer services at the press of a button. The availability of capital to broaden the reach is bringing down unit costs rapidly and scaling some of these offerings at a very rapid rate and, in turn, creating their own snowballs.

I think most of us would agree that an efficient system of ordering, tracking and getting diverse kinds of cuisines home-delivered in a reasonable time at a click does add value to a customer. A lot of us will be willing to pay for that service without batting an eyelid. Similarly, for a restaurant owner, there are myriad benefits to someone willing to eat the bought food at home and not crowd their seating space, especially in a high rental market like India. It might still not be efficient enough for smaller restaurants to have their own delivery person deliver food at multiple locations. I am sure there will be restaurants willing to give discounts for takeaways. But as a customer, if I make the effort to go to the restaurant, I might as well eat the food at the restaurant rather than get it packed.

Food delivery apps fill the void beautifully. But for them to grow and create a network, they need to go through an elongated period of cash burn, where they incentivise restaurants to register on their platforms, and at the same time incentivise customers with discounts to entice them to download their app ahead of the competition. So apart from getting a service and varied choices, I am also getting discounts. The consumer surplus for me is phenomenal. In the initial period, till the platform is not so strong that restaurants 'need' to be there, platforms give fantastic offers.

5. Consumer surplus is the difference in the perceived value of a product or a surplus, against what he is being asked to pay.

The restaurants get food delivered, get volumes and space, all for free or at very little cost.

Gradually, as the platform becomes bigger, it is able to charge for the services to the restaurant and in some cases even the consumer, creating a huge operating leverage. By this time they have managed to displace the existing delivery systems, have gotten restaurants used to increased volumes and they cannot do without these platforms. Similarly, the consumer is spoilt for choice and with offers he does not notice marginal differences in his food cost, even if it is higher than prices at the restaurant. The enormous consumer surplus on either sides (restaurant and the person ordering) starts reducing, but with the platform getting bigger, adds value and efficiencies in other ways, like reducing delivery timelines, larger bouquet of options to choose from, offers from payment gateways, loyalty programmes etc. Such businesses have a huge operating leverage and a snowball effect.

However, operating leverage is not a one-way traffic; it is also a double-edged sword. Imagine getting disrupted by a player who has even deeper pockets. He starts offering a better deal to restaurant owners and to consumers. He is willing to burn even more cash to grab market share. Suddenly one starts seeing pressure on the economics – restaurant owners start moving to another platform. You have to compete with this new platform on discounts offered and still a large pool of your customers start moving out. The food aggregator's revenue growth also starts getting impacted and the equity money is also not as easy to come by.

Foodpanda probably faced the same problem. With Zomato, Swiggy and Uber trying to grab market share, the quality of their platform started withering in the face of competition, with listings of restaurants that had closed down also appearing on their sites, and a trail of bad news – of letting people go, funding drying up – pretty much ended their dream run in the space. Covid may do the same for one or two more of these services as customers become increasingly reluctant to order food or order from new restaurants. The rapid rate of shut-down of restaurants and the inability to add new restaurants to the platform for a sustained period will adversely impact the growth metrics and the ability of some of these platforms to continuously raise money.

However, there is no denying that these food delivery apps have created a whole new industry and an opportunity for restaurant owners to optimise business models and create delivery-only models. In every major Indian city now we have restaurant businesses that really don't run any sit-down spaces and rely only on deliveries for their business.

Real estate broking went through a similar cycle, where a bunch of real estate brokers came up, like 99acres, makaan.com, housing.com, magicbricks.com, nobroker.in, commonfloor.com among others. Obviously, they provide a very important service to both sellers and buyers in the space. While sellers get a much wider reach and a platform to showcase their properties, it makes the price discovery and property hunting much easier for the consumer. He does not need to physically visit as many properties as he would have otherwise done in a different era.

It has also in many ways changed the brick and mortar brokers' behaviour. One remembers a time when brokers would first tire out a customer by showing him properties of extremely inferior quality for hours, and only then actually show a property that fits the bill. By sheer exhaustion, lack of options and the contrasts the buyer has seen earlier, he would feel somewhat pressured to close out the deal in a hurry, fearing that otherwise this property may also slip away. Online portals have put some of the power back in the hands of the consumer, so he will have the ability to quickly tell a broker not to waste his time, knowing fully well that there are other fish in the sea.

The prolonged slump in the real estate somewhat put paid to a lot of platforms in the space and many sank without a trace. Even market leaders like magicbricks.com, which is backed by the Times of India group, and 99 acres.com, which is backed by

Info Edge, are still struggling to break even after multiple years in existence. The good thing is that they have managed to get their metrics to a level where they can leverage any upswing in demand that may come to rapidly turn profitable and start generating free cash flows. The rich pool of customers, property investors, builders and broker networks that they have built are all ripe for leveraging. They are also creating a depth of options on the platform which rivals will take some time to match up to. Sometimes, not having large pools of money available for a sector can help create a more efficient and stronger business model. A lot will eventually depend on how some of the competitors and new entrants behave; when the real estate cycle turns will make a difference in terms of getting to the path of sustained profitability. As an investor, it is often much more advisable to take bets on sectors that are not on the favourable end of equity funding cycle. A down-cycle allows you to build a very strong platform without being charred by irrational market-share-grabbing behaviour of competitors.

Very often in these industries, the benefits of being a first mover are highly over-rated. If the industry is large enough, there will be multiple players and multiple investors who would want to have a piece of the business. The first ever search engine was called 'Archie', made in 1990 by Alan Emtage, Bill Heelan and Peter Deutsch, who were all computer science students at McGill University in Montreal, Canada. Google's first search happened much later, in 1998. Before Google, tech major Yahoo.com had a good search product, which was immensely popular, called Yahoo Search. Around early 2000s, Google started to become immensely popular and their page rank algorithms, along with minimalistic user interface, made it a raging hit and went on to subsequently create a tech space giant. As of September 2019, Google had a whopping 93% market share in the search business.

The 'winner takes all' nature of some of the consumer-facing internet businesses makes them probably one of the most exciting and at the same time riskiest businesses to invest in. Even if one identified search as the next big opportunity in mid-1990s, one would not have thought a newbie like Google could take on and beat a stronger incumbent like Yahoo.

High operating leverage businesses

Among traditional businesses, movie exhibition (theatre), hotels and restaurants have a similar operating leverage. They start making money only after a certain occupancy level. Most theaters would, for instance, have a break-even at 40-50% occupancy. The incremental cost of seating an additional patron is almost zero; further, he also contributes in terms of more F&B revenue. The same is true with hotels and restaurants. They have a high fixed cost, and every new patron, after meeting the fixed costs, adds disproportionately to the bottomline.

Apart from having their own store-wise break-even, these businesses also have an operating leverage in terms of brand, access to premier locations, loyalty programmes etc. It is fairly commonplace for a restaurant chain to do well over a decade and then suddenly when it starts to fall out of favour, the economics not only of an individual store but of the entire chain go for a toss. This is why the restaurant industry has traditionally seen a very high degree of mortality. According to a study done by the Ohio State University published in 2005, 60% of restaurants close or change ownership in the first year of operations and 80% within five years. The survivorship bias in liking a high operating leverage business is so huge that one often fails to gauge the extent of failures, shutdowns and risks associated with the business. Restaurants, like airline businesses, are an extremely glamorous business to be in and invariably do find willing investors to participate in their businesses.

As an investor who understands these equity funding cycles in a high operating leverage business, there are ways to improve your chances of winning and make money on these businesses. One would do well to find players who have already passed the first critical level of volumes and have the momentum in their favour. Secondly, it is equally important that the company one is backing is playing a niche and has competitive advantages beyond availability of money to play that niche. Trying to compete head-on with Amazon or Google in a space they compete aggressively in is very unlikely to yield great results. Thirdly, another very important aspect to look at while backing these plays is how they optimise their capital utilisation. If customer acquisition cost is increasing with every round of funding or if the money is increasingly being used to be deployed in unrelated capital hungry businesses, chances are the business will run out of money before it turns profitable.

Snowballs and raita

One of the largest payment companies in India has been spending extremely aggressively to increase penetration. They have done exceedingly well to increase market share and get customer loyalty. They have also entered into partnerships with the most popular taxi-hailing company and arguably have one of the most user-friendly products in the market. They tied up aggressively with billing companies and retailers, and gave customer cash back for bill payments, purchases etc. Although the operating numbers are not widely available, from financial numbers and user statistics, one feels that the client acquisition cost for every new customer is increasing for the platform. To top it all, the company started putting money on retailer aggregation and created a proxy retail marketplace of its own. Not only that, they have also created a platform for air bookings and hotel bookings and are competing with OTAs (online travel agencies) head-on in that space.

Personally, these businesses that want to be everything to everyone to get growth before getting their core business profitable, often turn out to be 'raita'[6] businesses. When the core

6. Raita is a curd-based gravy, which is colloquially used to imply a mess that spreads too thin and needs cleaning up.

business is not showing the ability to grow profitability on its own, and there is funding available, there is invariably a tendency amongst entrepreneurs to try add-more verticals, hoping for that to be an additional hook. The incremental investors' cash keeps getting deployed in building new hooks because the core business adds little value to customers without a cash burn. It is a fantastic platform and it has definitely changed digital micro-payments in India forever, but as an investor, the road to profitability – if they ever get there – will be a long and painful one.

However, some of the other businesses that have managed to stick to their core business and have progressively brought down client acquisition cost, strengthened the platform and got bargaining power in their favour, have a much better chance of not only surviving but becoming a dominant player for a long time to come. Lenskart is already a market leader in the eyewear space, having taken rapid strides in adding more muscle to the platform. Over the last few years, they enabled their door-to-door salesman to carry a large number of options in glasses, allowed for eye check-up at home, launched a private label brand called John Jacobs and opened more than 500 of its own eyewear retail stores.

With all this expansion happening, what they have managed to successfully do over the last year is to decrease losses while growing revenues. The cost of a pair of glasses bought from Lenskart is almost 40% cheaper than buying one from a neighbourhood store. Apart from being cheaper, most users report that on a like to like basis, the quality of lenses and frames is more often than not better than the neighborhood optician store. To top that, this business is still predominantly unorganised, and there is a distinct shift from unorganised players to organised players. According to a Deloitte report, they expect the eyewear industry to go from $ 7.4 billion in 2017 to $ 13.6 billion in 2024.

One would think that Lenskart has cracked a niche space, which is large enough to give them a long runway for growth and at the same time not large enough for the big boys to want them to burn too much cash. The ability to have a brand play and the demography's increasing preference for branded organised players make Lenskart an exciting proposition to back. To top it, the company has already demonstrated the ability to reduce new customer acquisition costs over the last couple of years, showcasing the positive benefits of operating leverage to play out in right earnest.

The way to understand the difference between Lenskart and the payment gateway is the analogy of stable equilibrium and unstable equilibrium in physics. A stable equilibrium is one where on being slightly moved from its position of rest, the object comes back to its original position, like a cone standing on its base. An unstable equilibrium is a situation where a slight movement from its position of rest increases the velocity in the direction of the disturbance, forcing the object to topple over, like a cone resting on its tip. The greater the number of variables required for a business to succeed, the more unstable the equilibrium becomes. Add cash burn and leverage to the mix, and sooner or later the chickens will come home to roost.

Another very beautiful example of operating leverage through an equity funding cycle is PolicyBazaar. The company, in 2018, had reached a stage where it was still doubling its customer base while reducing its losses. They are again in the financial services space, which is hyper-competitive, where one is competing with banks, insurance brokers, and direct sales from insurance companies and small agents who sell policies for additional income.

Even in a space like this, through their aggregation model, advisory and comparative analysis tools, they made a dent, and according to a market report, now hold 25% of the life insurance market. The follow-up and use of technology platforms for form filling, document proof and leverage with insurance companies is fantastic and in most cases their turnaround time to get a policy issued is even faster than the direct insurance purchases. Information on the websites is detailed enough for most people to understand and do an online purchase.

However, in June 2018 it got an infusion of $ 238 million from SoftBank. While all this was happening, the promoters started another business vertical called Docprime, which was to act as a healthcare services aggregator. Their client acquisition cost again started to go up and for every rupee they made, they were spending INR 1.7 as against INR 1.06 in FY 18. *(Source: Entrackr)* Suddenly, a great business with snowball effect kicking in, market share increasing and client acquisition cost reducing is at the risk of becoming a 'raita' stock because of availability of funding beyond what the business needs. The platform is stronger than ever, the services are top-notch and one just hopes that the road to profitability is not sacrificed indefinitely at the altar of topline growth.

Snowballs are generally those businesses that have a large consumer surplus, where customers are often willing to pay a value significantly higher than what the service provider is charging. As the platform becomes bigger, the consumer surplus also becomes bigger and creates a moat where others find it difficult to replicate it without indulging in a large cash burn. Being part of a smaller industry often limits incentives for a new player to indulge in that cash burn.

As an investor there is huge money to be made in chasing snowballs, but at the same time one has to be conscious of the risks of chasing snowballs. Too much of equity chasing snowballs can often make them too expensive, and if the management is not focused on operating metrics, it more often than not brings down the capital efficiency of the business they are growing. It is, hence, extremely important to understand the metrics the management is focused on improving with the money they are raising, the size of the industry and threats they foresee in the near future.

Indefinite topline growth plans may often be counter-productive unless accompanied by improvement in operating metrics and/or reduction in client acquisition costs. Similarly, getting into unrelated businesses or other crowded businesses can often help get more traffic to a platform but will probably continue to bleed the platform even more. If Netflix got into gaming services before they started making money on the streaming content business, would it have been better off? Probably that is the difference between a 'snowball' and a 'raita'.

Another kind of snowball that works well for industry leaders is the classic economies of scale. As the market leader starts getting bigger, his leverage with both vendors and distribution channels becomes better than that of the competition. The consumers are willing to pay more for the brand and per unit costs of overheads and advertising keep coming down with increasing volumes. To top that these companies invariably get significantly higher market multiples as compared to the smaller players. This allows them to acquire smaller players in this space through the equity route and the acquisition becomes value accretive from the very date of acquisition.

For example, Security and Intelligence Services India Ltd (SIS), the market leader in manned guarding business in India, trades at high multiples in high 20s and early 30s of their earnings multiples. It has consistently been growing its business by acquiring new businesses in related fields. It acquired dusters total solutions services – RARE Hospitality, UNIQ Detective &Security, Henderson Security – at a steep discount to its own listing trading multiple. These acquisitions instantly become value accretive even before the synergies and efficiencies of the acquisition started to kick in because of the difference in multiples of the target and acquirer. Being able to consolidate market share and have a larger market presence in an industry, which is fragmented and increasingly getting organised, give a huge tailwind for the growth of the company and its growth path.

The concept of a snowball and raita is relevant not only for corporations but also for us as human beings. The more we make an effort in building depth and competency, slowly but surely the snowball effect starts kicking in; one starts being perceived as an expert and more people start calling you for advice, improving your understanding of the subject even more. A raita approach sees you spreading yourself too thin across multiple activities, hoping something will stick.

9

Bull traps and Satraps

Investing as a vocation is a practice in continuing education. It is often easy to get snared in traps laid by promoters, the market or destiny. The traps could be hidden in the stock price, in the nature of the business or poor accounting and governance standards. There are some fairly common traps that even sophisticated investors often fall into.

Reverse compounding machines

Reverse compounding machines are one of the most dangerous businesses to be trapped in. These businesses incrementally keep losing their inherent shareholder value and at the same time the stock prices also come off rapidly. Both feed into each other to further accentuate the problem till the business itself becomes unsustainable.

These reverse compounding machines generally have either extremely high operating leverage or extremely high financial leverage and often both. The same leverage may have made them look like snowballs in the past but when the trajectory becomes uphill, the size of the ball makes the climb even tougher.

The NBFC (non-banking financial company) industry in India had a similar moment in 2018. With the IL&FS crisis spilling out into the open, the hitherto rapidly growing NBFC industry and smaller banks met their moment of truth. With the risk perception changing, access to capital for these businesses started becoming stiffer and costlier.

The financial services industry in many ways is a fiduciary business where trust in the management and balance sheet is an absolute must for businesses to grow and flourish. As the trust in the NBFC businesses and smaller banks started to erode, the quality of their lending books started to come under a deeper scrutiny by their providers of capital. Some NBFCs started to access the market for new pools of capital either by selling a part of their businesses, bond issuances or pledging promoters' capital.

The higher cost of capital and pledge of promoters' shares made the sustainability a bigger question mark. The loss of trust in one part of the business in a financial services business invariably scars other parts of the business. Also, the risk of default sometimes becomes so high for the overall business that promoters of these businesses are tempted to indulge in practices not completely above board.

For instance, one of the leading brokers and registrars in the country ended up pledging securities worth INR 2,300 crores of their clients with some of the lenders. The pledge was invoked, the owners of these securities went to court and the court restored ownership of the original shareholders. Whatever little hope the business had of surviving was put paid to with this blatant act of indiscretion.

Another NBFC which also had an AMC (asset management company), used its AMC to borrow large pools of money from. Probably, if all was good, they would have had access to other sources of capital, but when things go bad, in some ways one's hand is also forced towards indiscretion. Once these disclosures catch the public eye, trust evaporates and the castle keeps crumbling.

Two large private sector banks, which had created a tremendous amount of shareholder wealth in the past but had later got into bed with some dodgy promoters and were willingly lending and ever-greening their loans, were also devalued by the stock market. Ultimately, the regulator had to intervene and change the captains of the respective ships to help them get their house back in order.

Another mid-size bank, which was known for being able to make riskier loans and recover the same from the dodgiest cases, came under the scanner. The allegations of quid pro quo and ever-greening started flying thick and fast. To top it all, promoters and promoters' related entity had shares pledged in the market; the stock price started tumbling relatively fast and, ultimately, the government had to step in to stop a run on the bank and get a state-run bank to bail them out.

While all this was happening, and the prices of some of these stocks kept crashing to a third or a fourth of their all-time highs, there was always talk in the market in terms of what is the right price to buy them. How much more can these fall? The truth is there is very little one can do when a rapid reverse compounding machine starts chugging. Some businesses do survive, but they survive either through bankruptcies or through ownership change. It is virtually impossible to build or run a financial services business if both the customers and the providers of capital are losing faith in the person behind the wheel. Best is to stay as far away from these companies when the tide turns and if you have already invested in the past, cut your losses and run.

It's the time to IPO

The other very interesting trap is that of a capital market bound company. These companies have a greater vested interest in timing the market and sectoral upcycle to raise money. Typically, industries which do a large number of capital raise in one particular cycle, where not only the sector leaders but the also-rans are also able to raise capital at fancy valuations, are the sector to watch out for. If one would have invested in any of the real estate stocks in the 2006-2010 bull run, there is very little chance for any investor to have made money on them. More than a dozen real estate companies went public between November 2006 and October 2010. Some of the others raise money through institutional placements and private equity. After almost a decade, on an average, most of these companies are down anywhere between 50% and 99%. Only three of them have yielded positive returns, which have been paltry by any stretch of imagination.

The same is true for IPOs in the power sector in that period, another sector which saw tremendous interest from entrepreneurs to list and investors to invest in. More than half a dozen private sector power companies went public between 2007 and 2010, raising over INR 20,000 crores for the market. Six out of eight such companies are trading at a discount of over 90% from their IPO price and the other two are also down by half as of June 2020. Chasing IPO thematic stories have invariably led to huge value destruction for investors in general.

The problem is especially acute with businesses which need debt capital to sustain their business and growth. A high level of leverage in these capex hungry businesses invariably comes back to bite and only industry leaders are really in a position to raise capital in an adverse environment. It is a heady party when it is on and the fear of missing out (FOMO) is one of the biggest value destructors for a long-term investor. Those who managed to sit on cash and take money off the table eventually end up laughing all the way to the bank.

The fight to stay bankable

Another very common trap one falls into is of some companies who are dependent on external providers of capital, like on banks, to maintain their liquidity position. Corporates will often try to artificially inflate their profits to keep their businesses bankable and trustworthy. There are multiple ways to inflate profits, but the most common tool companies indulge in is showing simultaneous increase in net working capital and profitability. Increase in inventories and receivables while understating liabilities is one of the most commonplace ways to inflate profits. As an investor, it is important to look at cash flows very closely. If a business is showing profits but cash flows from operations are either not there or reducing, there is a problem. In best-case scenario, it shows a poor quality of earnings, where liberal credit is being given to get more market share, and in worst case scenario, it demonstrates poor accounting practices.

A mid-size company into manufacturing of white goods saw its PAT increase from INR 36 crores to INR 82 crores between 2011 and 2015. However, in each of these years, their cash flow from operating activities was negative. The receivables increased from INR 219 crores to INR 458 crores, and the inventory increased from INR 203 crores to INR 719 crores. After 2015, for another two years the inventory and the receivables kept increasing while profits became flat. The stock price went from INR 56 per share to over INR 300 per share, only to come crashing down as the shenanigans became too large to manage.

Similarly, a road construction and operating company saw its profit go from INR 16 crores to INR 87 crores between 2008 and 2016. However, the inventories went from INR 23 crores to INR 738 crores, and receivables went up from INR 87 crores to INR 652 crores. The capital work in progress also went from 0 to INR 860 crores. The stock price went from INR 32 per share in 2013 to INR 310 per share in 2015, only to come crashing down to INR 5 a share in the ensuing years.

Another cable company, which saw its profits increase from INR 28 crores in FY 2014 to INR 56 crores in FY 2016, went from being INR 60 per share in late 2015 to over INR 230 per share in January 2017. However, in those two years, the company saw its receivables go from INR 338 crores to INR 849 crores. Loans and advances went from INR 46 crores to INR 668 crores. Clearly, the profits being disclosed were not sustainable and the stock price came crashing down to single digits in no time.

More often than not such companies with compromised cash flows will end up either folding up their businesses, lose ownership control or will have to sell a substantial part of their businesses to a willing buyer. The purpose of such padding is to either be able to raise debt or to be able to raise equity from the market. Being able to show profits is absolutely critical for survival of this business. However, from an investor perspective, keeping an eye on cash flows can be one sure-shot way to escape the disaster that follows.

This is one of the likely reasons that investors often look at dividend payout track record very closely as a sanity check for actual profits. A business which is not really making cash is unlikely to pay out large sums in dividend or do a buy-back.

Poor capital allocators

An investor must look out for apparent conflicts of interest or a capital structure that is not investor friendly. A large company in a completely different commodity product line chose to diversify into thermal power plants. While the equity shares of the power company were held entirely by the promoters, they issued low-cost RPS (redeemable preference shares) and OCPS (optionally convertible preference shares) to the listed commodity company. Power plants in the best of times are long gestation and a risky project. This structure essentially meant that if the power plant takes off and makes money, the listed entity will get back its money invested in the form of RPS and OCPS, but will have no upside. However, if things go wrong, the money invested by the listed entity will come to naught. As things turned out, like the rest of the power industry, the power business continued to suffer and the listed entity ultimately had to write off its investments.

The same company also had another entity in which the promoters allegedly acquired almost half of the business for close to nothing, whereas the overall value of the business was in thousands of crores. These are, in a way, permanent red flags and investors will do really well to not associate themselves with promoters who indulge in such dubious practices. Promoters with dodgy past track records are never the best ones to partner with.

Even when the going is good, often owners of lots of quality businesses are tempted to get into unrelated capex intensive businesses. The primary reason is that they do not find a suitable outlet for re-investing their profits of a quality business. Satyam got into the real estate and infrastructure business, which effectively killed the otherwise profitable information technology business and had to be later bailed out by the Mahindras. Emami's foray into cement impacted their otherwise good FMCG business as well. To a much lesser extent, one of the most prolific and high quality FMCG company, ITC, also suffered from the classic reinvestment problem and diversified into hotels, agri products and apparel retail. Clearly, the returns from some of these diversifications are not in the same league as their core tobacco business.

The propensity for unrelated diversification is probably one of the reasons that a large rapidly growing FMCG does not get similar multiples as some of its peers.

Rear-view mirror investing

Another very common investing mistake is rear-view mirror investing. Investors are often tempted to bet on asset classes and sectors that have given them good returns in the past to deliver future returns also. Often that is a sure way to compromise portfolio returns. Investing in tech stocks when they have run up, or for that matter investing in real estate when they have quadrupled in five years, is a recipe for disaster. One has seen the trend in sector after sector and business after business. The trend is even more accentuated in capital-hungry stocks; the leverage and low-cost of capital, which work towards increasing valuations, work rapidly the other way round when cost of capital starts increasing and availability of capital starts to become scarce. Other sectors and asset classes also face the same challenge but probably the severity of the meltdown in those cases is more manageable.

We discussed earlier how it was virtually impossible for anyone to have made money on tech stocks on a longer-term basis if they had made a bet on them in 2000. Staying away from market noise can improve one's investing process tremendously, largely because of the fallacy of rear-view mirror investing. The mental bandwidth and bias it creates towards sectors that are the flavour of the time and the thrust on returns made in the immediate past often cripple the ability to look out for new exciting undiscovered themes in the market.

Satraps

Satraps are top players in leadership positions in either a small industry or a smaller geography. They are usually mid-cap and small-cap stocks that often escape the eye of an institutional investor. Illiquidity and lack of institutional interest in a stock are often friends of an investor, especially if the lack of interest is because of illiquidity and relatively smaller market capitalisation. The satraps of smaller industries often do not get their due from the market as market leaders in larger industries do. The good part is they rarely care. The business throws enough cash flows for them to care about the prevailing market price and they can continue to be investor-shy and do not feel the pressure to demonstrate quarter to quarter performance. This allows an investor to monitor performance over a period of time and increase stakes as conviction increases. Let us look at some satraps; how to identify them and why it makes sense to average up with them?

Astral Poly Technik is a market leader in making plastic pipes used in the construction of buildings. The company has shown tremendous growth over the period with the topline growing from INR 188 crores in FY 2009 to over INR 2,500 crores in FY 19. The profitability has been growing at a rate faster than the topline and the company has added building adhesives to its portfolio. The gross profit margin in each of the businesses has been consistently showing an improving trend; the working capital cycle is reducing, generating even more cash flows. Clearly, all the makings of a satrap in an industry which is also growing rapidly and taking market share from steel pipes and from unorganised players. These are typically the stocks that are worth averaging up till they hit the stratosphere.

We discussed how Prestige and Hawkins, satraps in the pressure-cooker industry, created enormous wealth in that space. Once they get discovered, institutional investors will invariably take the multiples to a different plane. The catch is to be able to identify them early on. Often these satraps are from lesser known consumer sectors or quasi consumer sectors. The best way to find these stocks is probably newspaper and television advertisements and your own experiences with respect to consumption patterns, brand preferences and market strength. As economies grow and purchasing power increases, more and more businesses start getting sold as a brand as against a commodity.

If a brand with strong recall value, but one which has not been using mainstream advertising aggressively, starts spending on television advertisements and hires brand ambassadors, it is usually a sign that they are reaching a critical mass where the advertisement spends and brand creating activities have started to pay for themselves. As the number of units sold increases, the unit cost of doing mainstream advertising is often lower than pushing the product through sales incentives and offers. Whether it was Astral or Prestige, they all started to do mainstream advertising and hiring brand ambassadors when they hit that mark.

Another example of a similar success story is Relaxo, a relatively strong brand in footwear space, with a good market presence in the hawai chappal segment. They beat a lot of stronger incumbents like Bata and Liberty to deliver growth, which outstripped the stronger incumbents. The company went from INR 306 crores turnover in FY 2008 to INR 2,292 crores in FY 19, consistently improving on margins and profitability. The stock price, which consistently used to be below INR 20 per share till 2012, went up to over INR 800 per share in a span of seven years. They also hired Bollywood superstar Salman Khan for their advertising in 2012. If one would have seen the increasing market spend and its effect on profitability since then, there was enough runway to make money. Incidentally, Astral had also signed Salman Khan in 2014 – the stock went 6x since then.

The real thing to identify is if increasing marketing spend and hiring a brand ambassador is happening at the right time in the business when the volumes can sustain it. Also, we have often seen celebrity endorsements in B2B plays, normally those are done for personal satisfaction of promoters rather than for the company. However, tracking media activity in your daily newspaper can give better stock ideas than hearing a lot of investor advice on business channels or looking at a business daily.

Sliver satraps

Certain satraps really don't need celebrity endorsements or large expenditures to become bigger. They manage to do it based on other advantages, like strength of the platform, technology and relationships. One business that readily comes to mind is TeamLease. TeamLease is arguably one of the largest temp staffing companies in the country. As of March 2020, it had over 3,500 clients and was employing 2.2 lakh associates. The beauty of the business was its low margins. Let's call these businesses, which are market leaders in low-margin industries, 'sliver satraps'. The company operated on wafer-thin margins of less than 2%. To be able to provide quality, reliable and ongoing sustained services to large clients at these kinds of margins created an entry barrier very difficult to replicate. The size allowed them to invest heavily in technology and they gradually started moving their PAT margins north of 2%. For a very low margin business it meant an exponential jump in their profits and surplus cash flows.

Clearly, this is one of the businesses to be seriously impacted by Covid, which will impact its balance sheet in the short run and profitability in the mid-term. However, with the quality of management and the platform they have created, one would believe they would tide through this as well and, if anything, this will give opportunities for investors to get a pie of this wonderful business at a cheaper price. This will also make weaker players vacate the marketplace, and give bargaining power to the business when businesses want to scale back to their usual capacity levels. Also, scarred by this sudden drop in demands, there may be a tendency for a lot of companies to employ a large pool of temporary staff rather than take more labour on their own payrolls.

A low-margin business is very difficult to build, and once built, even more difficult to compete against. TeamLease is certainly not a satrap I would want to bet against!

We discussed Gravita in earlier chapters, another example of a classic sliver satrap variety, with extremely low margins and market leadership position in lead recycling industry. Other very interesting examples of sliver satraps are payment gateway companies like Visa and Mastercard. In a brick and mortar world they were a classic low-margin business with distribution and network strength almost impossible to dislodge. They added value to the merchant in terms of getting more footfalls, credit to customers and lower cash management hassle. They added value to the customers with free credit, loyalty programmes and card-specific privileges. They also added value for banks issuing these cards, by not having to create their own point of sale (PoS) network and distribution chains. All this for an overall cut of 1% to 2.5% of the sale value, including payout to banks and the PoS equipment provider.

However, what was a low-margin-difficult-to-dislodge business in the brick and mortar era became a relatively high-margin business in the digital era. With online payment processing, multiple payment gateways and business models carving their own niche through alternative and much lower cost payment mechanisms. In fact, many payment gateways don't charge any money on extending credit and giving working capital limits for trade finance to them and to their vendors. No one would want to bet against the might of Visa and Mastercard, but one would think that a lot of new players are increasingly going to eat both into their margins and into their market share.

Another satrap which has created a strong business in a niche category and also has a huge snowball effect kicking in is the B2B listing company IndiaMART. They have created a fantastic B2B platform, which not only enables users to list their products and services but to also get quotes and bids from suppliers. They have over 67 million product listing and pretty much anything commercially sold or bought is listed on their platform. The number of queries and registered buyers on the platform runs into tens of millions and the network effect that has created is hard to dislodge.

Over the years, the quality of product listing has been improving dramatically with pictures, pricing and product details being given on the platform. They are continuously adding to the platform with new SaaS (software as a service) offerings, payment protection and improved user interface. Back-end search engines and call centers are optimised to enable customers' access to most active and most relevant suppliers.

Both the number of paying subscribers and average revenue per user are steadily increasing and the marketplace strength of the platform is rapidly consolidating. To top it all, being a subscription business, customers pay upfront and often for multiple years, which means that there is no breakage or a negative working capital in the business. The cash flows are stronger than revenue. With a large pool of cash sitting on the balance sheet, they are well positioned to meet any adverse development and at the same time scale up their business. Perhaps the biggest challenge from here on will be to manage the reinvestment risk of the cash pool sitting in the balance sheet and to build more flanks around the current businesses.

A new satrap takes over

An interesting theme for investors is when they have been playing in an interesting domain and the incumbent satrap is seen losing its way. This may happen in the case of a conglomerate wanting to willingly cede ground in an industry as the focus industry is not large enough or because of generational change, where the next generation is not so bullish on that particular business or general management ineptness. This is the time the market starts to open up for challengers who are looking to become the new satrap of the industry.

For instance, the demise of Kingfisher Airlines and Jet Airways, and the rapid decline of Indian Airlines have created a window for InterGlobe Aviation Ltd (IndiGo) to grow at a very rapid rate. The sales of IndiGo went from INR 1,133 crores in FY 2008 to a whopping INR 28,497 crores in FY 2019; in an industry where the competition was suffering from debt and losses, IndiGo was making a profit of over INR 3,000 crores with a dominant market position. With a well-capitalised balance sheet, the business is likely to further consolidate its dominance and market position over the next few years. Having a strong and well-capitalised balance sheet in a high-operating leverage business is absolutely critical to survive turbulent times. Aviation is one sector that more often than not invariably sees a very tough cycle almost every decade. As owners or shareholders in this business, it will take a very brave man to back a leveraged player.

Another very interesting example in a commodity space is that of Ballarpur Industries Ltd (BILT), which till FY 2014 was a market leader in the wood-based paper business with a turnover of over INR 5,000 crores. BILT invariably commanded a premium over the competitor and was over two and a half times the size of its next competitor. However, the leverage at the group level started to impact their paper business also, and the company went into distress. Their competitors like JK Paper, Seshasayee Paper and West Coast Paper improved their margins in the following period, and JK Paper also consolidated its market position. It will, in all probability, become the next satrap of the industry. In spite of the increased debt on the books due to acquisition and the commodity nature of the product, it might be a bet worth taking on. Usually, the claimant to the throne in industries like these that need resources and infrastructure are other well-entrenched incumbents.

Similarly, as Crompton's electricals business also started getting impacted by the group-level issues, players like Havells took market share in the fan business and Symphony increased its market share in the cooler business. For Havells the fan business was just a top-up on its sale in a multi-product business, but for Symphony, which largely plays in the cooler segment alone, the uptick in turnover was phenomenal. It went from a topline of INR 268 crores in FY 13 to INR 711 crores in FY 19. The profit also grew more than three times. Such group-level stress in market leaders in a segment is a good time to try and see if there is a clear player who can lay claim to the throne. With a relatively strong Insolvency and Bankruptcy Code now in place, the ability of bankers to have their say and enforce management change has substantially increased. This brings a greater degree of confidence to investors in calling out a management change.

Clearly, the benefits for a distribution channel oriented company are disproportionately more when it comes to increasing market strength vis-à-vis a commodity player. A branded product is able to push its products with lesser discount, extend lesser credit and has a perceptible hold on consumer preference. Many of these benefits are significantly reduced in commodities like paper, but even in these, market presence enhances the bargaining power of the market leader.

While identifying satraps and putting money behind them, it is extremely important that we take our time in allocating capital and establishing track record. Indian corporate history is replete with examples of false gods who have only flattered to deceive.

With track record one must be willing to average up and allocate more capital. As an investor, it is one of the most satisfying things to be able to average up with improving performance – and extremely profitable too.

10

Capital Allocation and Risk Mitigation

Investing as an activity is fraught with risk. There are risks not only if you invest in equity, but also if you invest in debt securities or even if you don't invest at all. In debt investing, inflation can outstrip the returns you get and a rising yield may impact your real returns or can even make them negative. To top it all, there is credit risk where the borrower may or may not be able to pay back the principal in part or in full. Similarly, sitting on cash or parking it in a bank in a world that is inflationary will invariably lead to negative real returns. Even government-backed securities are not immune to risks of inflation and gradual value erosion.

Some of the safest investments, i.e retiral schemes like provident fund and public provident fund, are also not immune to inflation. The government also from time to time adjusts yields on these funds. Further, most of these schemes have a lock-in, which essentially means that a lot of times it may not be possible for you to access the money when you need it or when you spot really good opportunities to invest. It is very commonplace for salaried individuals to have continuing investments in retirals at a rate lower than their home loans. This essentially means that while one has his own money to buy a house, he is parking it in a deposit which yields lower returns than what he is paying banks to borrow.

It probably does not make any sense but such behaviour is triggered by two things. Firstly, there is a need to manage cash flows. One may not have enough money at the time of buying the house and the corpus gradually builds, and it appears much easier to pay EMIs (equated monthly installment) from your salary than to take out your money. Secondly, most people have different buckets for their money. Most of these retirals are looked at as a security cover or are earmarked for a child's education, marriage etc.

Real estate also goes through its own ups and downs and very often gives no or negative returns even over extended periods of time. So if one invests in real estate by taking home loans at a rate higher than the interest one is getting on his own investments, the negative carrying cost of those loans can be significant. In India, usually it is often much cheaper to rent a house than to buy a house, except for periods when one sees rapid capital appreciation.

Capital allocation to equity

There is enough literature to show that if one looks at investing as a multi-decade activity, equity investments beat all other asset classes hands down in terms of annualised returns. Even if one accounts for leakages due to brokerage and asset management fee of mutual funds, which do make a dent to annualised returns, it will still outstrip other asset classes in terms of returns.

The truth is the risk of not investing in equities is way more than the risk of investing in equities. We had discussed earlier how INR 1 lakh invested at 15% yields almost two and a half times the amount that INR 1 lakh invested at 10% does over a period of twenty years. In India making a 15% nominal return on equities is not very difficult and with simple capital allocation strategies even a passive mutual fund investor can hope to achieve that. However, making 10% on risk-free debt is virtually impossible over a period of time. *Anyone advising you to not invest in equities for the purpose of security is stripping off a huge sum from your future self.* Further, simple rupee cost averaging techniques like SIP can easily help a passive investor beat market (index) returns. In the long run only three things matter: i) returns, ii) capital allocation, iii) risk mitigation.

While doing capital allocation, one must not worry about long-term end use. If there is surplus money which you do not need for the next five to six years, your investment strategy should be independent of end use. You will invariably see lots of very smart people putting in money in buckets for long-term end use, like a college fee fund for their unborn child or marriage fund for their kids, or a fund for their retirement homes. Mostly, they want these investments to be secure and end up parking them in fixed income bearing asset classes.

The inherent risk of the value of savings being inflated out and compounding at a low rate in such long-term investment strategies is a dampener, which seriously impedes wealth creation and often the end objectives. The cost of end objectives, like the retirement home or a wedding, often ends up growing at a rate faster than the asset pool in which the money is being invested.

As a Polycycle Investor, one should not invest large sums of long-term money in locked up debt securities. The opportunity cost of money not being available when the market presents an opportunity is way higher than the return long-term debt can give. It is balderdash to believe that debt money locked up for a decade is more secure than equity investments.

This does not mean that one should not have investments in debt. Depending on an individual's investible corpus, every investor should invest in a relatively diversified asset pool comprising equities, debt and whatever other asset class he likes, whether real estate, gold etc. However, there should be relative flexibility to move from the other asset classes to equity. Since equity gives the best returns in the long run, one needs to have the highest allocation of their investible surplus in equities. For individuals who still have more than a decade of earning life ahead of them, this number should ideally be above 50%, and for those who have a larger investible surplus than what they need to maintain their standard of living, the number might as well be closer to 80%.

Often when markets crash, equities are perceived to be riskier. The truth is actually just the opposite. A softer cheaper market has a much higher margin of safety than an exuberant market growing rapidly. In a volatile but soft market, a good investor is in a much better position to pick up bargains than he would be in an exuberant market. What is required is to have mental models to take out the money from an exuberant market, put it in secure debt securities and be able to reinvest it back at significantly lower levels. It is almost impossible to time the market tops or bottoms, but it is not very difficult to know when it is too expensive or too cheap. Similarly, it is relatively easier to assess if individual stocks are cheap or expensive than to have a blanket view of the market as a whole.

Armed with an understanding of the cycles, one is in a much better position to time exits and entry from/into a stock than he would otherwise be. For instance, one of the mental models one can work with is if one can expect both earnings and multiples to expand in this stock over the next five years. If the answer to that question is yes, it is worth entering the stock.

Another question I often end up asking myself at the stage of exit is: can either the multiples of this company or the earnings of the company go to a half from their current levels over the next four to five years? If the answer to either of these two questions is yes, probably one should look for an exit.

While answering these questions, one should not imagine extreme buoyancy or an extremely pessimistic market environment. Also, historic multiples though a guide, often start to become irrelevant after a stock is 'found' by institutional investors, and there is always a possibility that a particular stock may not go back to historical lows. Like a mid-cap once found may not retrace back to its old multiples similarly, a company which has fallen out of favour because of corporate governance issues or a sector on a terminal decline, may never get the multiples it got in its heydays. As an investor, one needs to be cognizant of these structural changes while evaluating long-term multiples.

Like one needs to have mental models to enter or exit a particular stock, similarly one needs to have mental models in terms of when to take money off the table and when to put more money into the market. One of the ways to look at it is the historic high for Sensex PE multiples as an exit or entry threshold. A mid-twenties Sensex PE is a good threshold to start monetising investments in equity, and a mid-teens PE is a good time to start putting in larger doses of capital back into the market. A model to vacillate between 40% in bull markets and 100% of the investible surplus in bear markets is a fairly conservative and good model to work with.

If opportunities are mouth-watering and one is able to find high-quality companies at rock-bottom prices, good quality companies at high dividend yield (say >5%), it does not hurt to leverage and even allocate up to 150% of their investing surplus, depending on one's risk appetite. Like we discussed in earlier chapters on cycles, the delta of being able to put money in a depressed market and take out money in a bull market is huge over a multi-decade investing activity.

There is a reason why most of your financial advisors would ask you to always stay invested in the market. Their commissions depend on the AUMs (assets under management) they manage, and if someone takes money out in a bull market, their commissions come down. Not only do their commissions come down, they always fear that your money, once it moves, may never come back. Also, this is the easiest time to convince most investors to stay invested. You just need to show them the rear-view mirror of good performance. Investors would have made fantastic returns on their equity portfolio over the previous two to three years and will be more than inclined to believe that such returns are sustainable over a longer period of time. Although it may sound foolhardy to some, if you trust your advisor enough, you can better your portfolio returns significantly by paying him a similar fee for taking a cash position. This would align his incentives with yours and will not make him stay invested when he believes that the markets have become overpriced.

Apart from taking a call on allocation to equity and other asset classes, one also needs to take a call in terms of allocation within the portfolio, both from the risk perspective as well as relative valuation perspective. In any market there are always mini-bubbles or areas of absolute or relative overvaluation. One of the heuristics to identify overvalued sectors is the capital market activity in that space. Any space seeing a large number of capital market transactions is either distressed or overvalued. By and large, it may be advisable to stay away from a large allocation in those sectors. Another heuristic is media and expert noise. A sector that is being discussed within the investor community and television experts for over a year has probably already over-run its steam.

Having said that, heuristics are only a leading indicator and not a substitute for understanding the business, valuations and the environment they operate in. After one has identified sectors of potential overvaluation, one still needs to dispassionately assess and take a call on exit. Sometimes, it makes sense to exit even very high quality players if their price exceeds intrinsic value by over 50% to allocate them in areas of relative undervaluation. A lot of times investors think of capital allocation and asset allocation as a binary exercise. In reality, it rarely is. Most investors with a decent investible surplus will have allocation in multiple asset classes at all points of time – the trick is to have the right balance among those assets.

Similarly, while doing asset allocation between sectors and companies, one needs to be reasonably diversified. One should never allocate disproportionate amounts on one sector or one company irrespective of the perceived undervaluation. Investing is an exercise fraught with risks and over a longer period of time even the best of investors get humbled on even their high conviction ideas. A disproportionately high allocation in any one stock or asset can cause permanent damage to capital. As a thumb-rule, 15% for a stock and 25% for a sector look like a reasonable upper cap.

Understanding your own game

There was a gambler who had a very interesting betting strategy. He used to have a 'double or nothing' bet on a cards game. He would start with making a small bet and keep on doubling the bet amount till he wins. Every time he won, he would again start with a low bet and keep repeating the process. If one has a large enough corpus to do it, there is no upper cap and the marketplace is fair, one is unlikely to walk out losing anything with this kind of a strategy over a longer period of time even if you are wrong four times out of five.

Many stock market investors, especially traders, do just the opposite. Every time they win, they up their bet for the next trade. If you keep doing that over and over again, it is very unlikely that you will have your principal intact even if you are right four out of five times.

Investing in equities is a strategic game; one needs to have a conviction that if one continues to play this game over and over again, for say a hundred times, what are the chances that he may have a permanent damage to a portfolio. If there is a significant probability of having a large loss if the game is played over a hundred times, probably you are in the wrong game. Over an investor's investing timeline, chances are those high risk events will happen at least four to five times, and if adequate risk mitigation strategies are not in place, it could be a potential recipe for disaster. For instance, if there is a permanent loss of capital of even 50% of your portfolio value, you would need 100% returns to just break even. The entire loss and getting back can easily take away a decade of portfolio returns. One needs to play the game in a manner that when you win, you win big and when you lose, you lose small and you ensure that you never have to go back home with empty pockets.

Similarly, as a predominantly equity investor, one should avoid large pools of capital being deployed either in locked-up securities or high-risk securities. Locked-up debt can be extremely costly, causing a huge loss of opportunity. Also, market presents best opportunity when credit is not available. Lots of poor credit quality investments will either delay or will not be able to pay up when you need money the most.

Lend carefully, borrow rarely

Money taken out from the market because of overvaluation should ideally be invested in high-credit, high-liquidity instruments, like bank deposits, high credit quality liquid funds etc. A paradoxical thought, but as an equity investor it often makes sense to move to debt when interest rates are low and move to equity when interest rates are high. A low interest rate scenario is a sign of stability and confidence in the business environment, which often leads to overvaluation in equity markets. Conversely, a high-interest rate scenario is often a sign of panic in the market and limited ability of institutions to take credit risks. A high-capital cost scenario can create a sustained period of undervaluation and opportunities in the market. If one looks at the graphs below, the high real interest rates scenario is mostly accompanied by a low-capital market returns and vice versa. As the interest rates start heading south, the capital markets start going up.

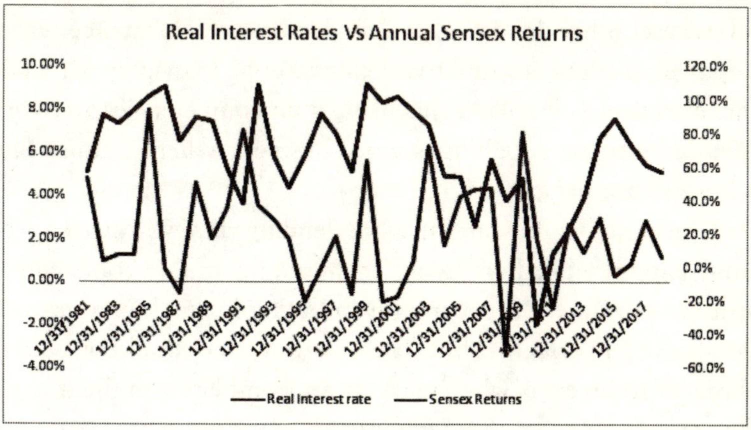

Secondly, it makes very little sense to invest significant amounts in high-yield debt securities. By definition the borrowers of high-risk debt securities are of a risky variety and there will be liquidity risk, credit risk or both. As a game which one plays multiple times, one can almost be certain that during your investing lifetime, some of those borrowers will default. As someone who holds a portfolio of debt securities, one may still have a chance of making money for an extended period of time, but if overall market conditions turn acutely adverse, the rate of default will invariably be higher than the incremental benefits one gets from it.

Often, financial institutions whose own cost of capital is higher than the competition, get completely priced out in the competitive high-quality credit market, and have to increasingly play on a riskier turf. As a retail investor or an investor with limited investible surplus, it makes very little sense to play in this market for a few percentage points of yield. Backing lenders, playing in this turf is even riskier. In addition to the risks they take on riskier assets, they are themselves highly leveraged, so a problem in a relatively smaller part of their lending book can potentially erode the complete net worth of the lender.

There are, however, exceptions. There are certain lenders who make up for their higher costs of funds by lending in a specialised field where other lenders are not lending; for instance, farm equipment lenders, automotive lenders, gold loan players, trade finance specialists etc. They may have built competencies, network and underwriting capabilities in a business where mainstream lenders are not present.

One needs to be careful while lending, but you need to be doubly careful while borrowing. It should invariably come with a statutory warning: 'Borrowing for investing in stock markets can be hazardous to your wealth'. The only time one should be willing to borrow to invest is when markets are completely in the dumps. *One of the best things about investing in stock markets is that your downside is capped at 100% while your upside is unlimited. The second best thing is that a long-term investor has time as his ally. He can choose to exit when the opportunity presents or continue to hold the stock till the conviction in the business itself is there.*

A levered investor loses both these advantages. He may have to sell a good stock at a price he does not agree to, because his leverage has taken away his ability to stay put and his losses could be more than the original money invested in stocks; there is a carrying cost of debt he borrowed, plus the value of the money invested could be less than what it was when he borrowed the money. Often a bad market comes with illiquidity in other asset classes like real estate, increasing interest rates and job losses. On top of that, if one is saddled with debt and a portfolio which is worth significantly lower than the amount invested, it is definitely an undesirable situation to be in. It is like being between a rock and a hard place, with the interest gradually crushing you against the rock. An event like this not only has a financial cost, it often has personal costs in terms of mental health, disturbed family life etc. Clearly not worth the bargain.

Futures and options can also have a similar impact on your portfolio, as your exposure is multiple times the amount being committed for the trade. A lot of futures and options traders ascertain their competency and success in terms of the number of times they are right vis-à-vis the number of times they are wrong. But the bigger risk is: how much they would lose in extreme volatility if they are wrong? Often, like most traders, everyone has a target amount of money they wish to make on a trade; there are stop-losses also, but gyrations of markets in extreme volatility can make mincemeat of these stop-losses and can take away years of trading profit and more in a relatively short span of time.

Leverage is like a reverse compounding machine for your portfolio, the same way leverage is a reverse compounding machine for a real estate or a commodity company stuck in an adverse cycle. You know that cycle will eventually turn, but a leveraged company may go bankrupt or could seriously erode its net worth by then. Leverage makes time a ticking time bomb. In investing, time is a very precious ally and a very dangerous foe. Not being dependent on stocks for your livelihood and not having an interest clock ticking significantly improves your investing process and allows you to time your entry and exit purely on merit.

As a multi-decade investor, one has to look at investing as tending to a tree. One needs to keep watering it, put it out where there is fresh air and sunlight, look at it once in a while, pluck its fruits when they are in season, and the tree grows nice and handsome. Once in a while prune the dry and rotting branches and make sure you save them from dangerous weeds and fungus. Your portfolio is fairly similar – with some basic care and interventions, given the right environment, it will grow with minimal effort. However, one has to protect it from risks of leverage and concentration and needs to prune the dead branches once in a while. Bigger environmental risks like market cycles are not in the control of the investor, but one has to still make sure that the shelter is strong enough to protect them till the storm passes.

Choosing the right partner

Apart from the general risks of poor capital allocation,

concentration and leverage, there is another huge risk in partnering with the wrong set of promoters. Promoters who have a checkered track record of rewarding shareholders or who have defaulted in paying back lenders are generally not worth backing. Another housekeeping check worth doing is if there is a churn in the senior management, especially the CFOs (chief financial officer) of a company. Generally, a churn in the senior management of a company is a sign of either poor corporate governance or poor health of the company or both. As Warren Buffett once famously said, 'There is never just one cockroach in a kitchen.' If the promoter is crooked, it will show in multiple ways. These promoters generally reward shareholders only when they are looking to do a capital raise, and treat them with absolute disdain afterwards. One would do well to look at a minimum of five-year track record of good governance before trusting a management.

A dairy company had seen a steep fall from over INR 180 per share to INR 32 per share in the span of about two months in 2011. In 2011 they were looking to do a fund raise through institutional investors and the stock price was running up prior to fund raise. Then some diligence issues cropped up. They appointed reputed auditors and got a forensic audit done to establish market confidence in the company. The objective was to do a fund raise again, and the stock price in 2016 again went back to over INR 160 per share. Market perception of the company continued to be choppy.

Right on cue, the company got over INR 500 crores from a reputed NBFC in 2016. All this time the reported PAT of the company kept on growing. It went from under INR 50 crores to INR 200 crores in 2017. But one look at the cash flows would have shown that the increase in profitability was coupled with an even sharper increase in receivables. Finally, in 2018, the NBFC took the company to the National Company Law Tribunal (NCLT) for recovery and the sole bidder for the company was an FMCG major with a total bid of INR 130 crores. The stock price of the company crashed to below INR 5 per share.

This example covers so many aspects of what we have discussed above. An NBFC took position in a company with suspect corporate governance to make a higher yield. It is extremely difficult to make money on such a bet. Similarly, if a company has had a track record of having suspect books and dubious stock market track record in terms of price movements, it is best to stay away from such a company at any price. It will take a very lucky man to make money on such a bet whether it is debt or equity.

Similarly, there are always risks in partnering with groups known to be owned by politically exposed persons (PEP). During the coal mining scam, lots of coal blocks were given away to entrepreneurs looking to set up power plants. A bunch of awardees were entrepreneurs who were relatives or known to be very close to the incumbents in the government. Some of these companies didn't even have a track record of being in the power business. Later the Supreme Court set aside all these coal block allocations. One such company which went public in 2008 to raise over INR 800 crores currently has a market capitalisation of less than INR 50 crores. The stock has virtually lost all its value since its IPO days.

While there is always an odd chance of making lots of money in the short run in a stock run by a dubious promoter or a PEP, the risk of rapid and permanent loss of capital in such businesses is way too high to overlook. As a multi-decade long-term investor, one would always prefer to partner with high quality promoters.

Anyway, allocation to businesses that are subject to rent-seeking behaviour can always turn out to be a bit dicey. One should not allocate disproportionate amounts to industries that are too dependent on the government for allocation of resources like scarce mineral resources. Even if the company one chooses to back is run by a fantastic promoter, the competitive and regulatory landscape can be queered by companies playing dirty.

The only way to create a healthy growing portfolio is to be extremely conscious of risks which may erode the capital permanently. Managing risks and getting your capital allocation strategy right, to that extent, is even more important than having the right stock-picking skills. An average stock picker with a robust capital allocation framework will beat a fantastic stock picker with poor capital allocation and risk management skills by a yawning margin.

Another very common mistake people make is to chase companies in deep stress when they have fallen 70-80% or more from their highs. If a large market-cap company has corrected that much, probably there is a very good reason for the same. Even from those levels, your loss in such a stock can be 100% of your invested value. The Indian stock market is full of examples of 'abyss' stocks, which fell into an abyss and then fell a bit more and then just vanished. Betting on those stocks, at best, is a gambling activity and not an investing activity.

11

India – A Polycycle Bonanza!

As an equity market investor, one feels extremely fortunate to be an investor in India in this century. We are in a happy situation where India is rapidly moving from low middle income economy to a genuinely middle economy. We have a demography that is young and aspirational, a community that has always put a premium on children's education and inculcating a habit of savings. The middle class of India has more economic resilience than the middle class in most countries who are in a similar per capital income bracket and the resilience that developed countries had when they were at this stage of their economic journey. The sheer size of the economy, the population and its regional and cultural diversity create an opportunity for multitudes of business models to thrive and grow. The diversity allows investors to have diverse styles and diverse themes to play on, making the Indian capital market a stock picker's delight.

While the pace of change in governance and strengthening of institutions may feel painstakingly slow, if you have a multi-decadal approach, there is no denying that over the last three decades India has come a long way in terms of regulatory framework, ease of doing business, unlocking the entrepreneurial hunger of the population and progressive laws. Each of the pillars of democracy – whether it is judiciary, executive, legislative or the media – have become more mature and, at the same time, have a greater public scrutiny. Of course, there is ample room for improvement, but the journey has surely begun.

Development of capital markets

It is important to disconnect oneself from the daily onslaught of news to get a sense of what India has achieved over the last three decades. The capital market depth has increased multi-fold and retail investors have taken to mutual fund investing, especially through the SIP mode, in a very aggressive manner. Access to increasingly cheaper equity capital for the country is a huge value creator. A basic study of discounted cash flows (DCF) will help one in understanding the value creation that happens when the cost of capital moves from say 12% to 9%. The value of the business becomes multi-fold even with zero growth. The capital market regulator, the Securities and Exchange Board of India (SEBI), and the respective stock exchanges have been extremely proactive and forthright to curb malpractices like rigging, insider trading and fronting from the market to protect the interests of small traders and investors.

Disclosure norms for access to capital markets and the presentation of financial statements and audit process are getting more conservative and transparent, and the perpetrators of large frauds are being brought to book and their businesses being taken away through insolvency procedures.

Regulators in other domains, like AMFI (Association of Mutual Funds in India), are doing their bit to increase market depth and get more and more investors attracted to the capital markets. A relatively stable but depreciating currency regime and a focus on domestic manufacturing will create new businesses and more employment. The infrastructure, though still extremely poor, has taken strides in terms of the development of roads, power sector, ports, airports and railways. On an ongoing basis the pace of some of these changes may look slow, but if one compares it in terms of decades, much seems to have changed.

Robust democracy, policy checks and balances

The Indian democracy has also matured and its electoral process, which was earlier riddled with booth capturing, violence and malpractices, now conducts elections with unprecedented transparency and institutional control. The benefits of these checks and balances are often not understood very clearly, as the direct benefits of these are difficult to demonstrate. But for the country these institutions are a treasure trove. The ability of incumbents to continue to hold on to the reins of power by manipulating the electoral process is increasingly coming down.

One would think that based on growth the country has seen over the last few decades, India has largely averted the risk of being a low-income trap economy[7]. The fiscal responsibility charter and focus to maintain that over longer periods will also ensure that India does not fall into a permanent debt trap. At the policy level, both on the fiscal side and the monetary policy side, the country has done well to manage risks. Errors in fiscal and monetary policy, if any, have probably been on the conservative side rather than on the aggressive side. In spite of conservatism in both these policies, the country has shown an ability to grow at an annualised growth rate of over 6% for over two decades now. Clearly, this would have not been possible if some of the fundamentals of the country were not sound.

India has always been a country of savers; even while being a low mid-income economy our domestic savings rate is at 30%. Just as a comparison, high income countries like the US and the UK are in high teens in terms of their domestic savings rate. Historically, Indians have parked their savings mostly in real estate and jewelry. With GST and demonetization one can see a very rapid rate of financialisation of these savings. The money is moving into banks,

7. A low income trap economy is one which is consistently at a low per capita GDP level and due to inadequate capital formation and investment levels, consistently struggles to grow their per capita GDP

fixed income securities and equity markets. The hitherto parallel economy is shrinking rapidly. India always had a large parallel economy, which managed to evade taxes by trading in cash and completely by-passed the formal tax structures. With a value-added tax structure, the incentive to evade tax is rapidly decreasing and more and more businesses are falling under the tax net. With a high GDP growth rate and the rate of formalisation of economy, tax buoyancy will create surplus resources for the governments to deploy. To ensure better compliance, the government has also incentiviszd businesses by bringing down corporate tax rate to 25%, and for new manufacturing industries to 15%. These are unprecedented low tax rates in the Indian context, and will further fuel the spirit of entrepreneurship.

Like investors compound their portfolios, countries also compound their strengths and have a huge snowball effect over a longer period of time. A few decades of compounding the GDP over 6% can mean a dramatic change to lifestyles within a generation (say 25 years). The surpluses generated, infrastructure created, defence bolstered and access to healthcare and education have multiplier effects for the economy and the population living in it. The deprived population moves to middle income and the middle income groups move to higher middle income and high income brackets. The fillip to consumption and many other businesses of this demographic transition creates immense value for shareholders of good businesses.

Just under three decades ago, if one would have travelled along the countryside, one would have seen a large number of mud houses with thatched roofs. The last quartile of the population would often struggle to get two square meals and clothes to cover their bodies. India, though still a very poor country, has come a long way in addressing the abject poverty levels of those times. The growth in economy and the welfare policies of successive governments have taken out tens of crores from abject poverty.

Stock picker's delight

India is a country of entrepreneurs and of much history. A study of the sheer variety of businesses that exists and their individual strengths is an education in itself, and building a depth of understanding in these invariably presents more and more opportunities and themes to get excited about. The more the diversity, the more the scope for mid-size businesses to carve out their own niche to fight the big boys. For instance, the ready-to-drink beverages market has been a virtual duopoly in most of the large markets. But in India lately, the regional ready-to-drink players are giving the giants a run for their money and growing at almost twice the rate as the big boys *(source: The Economic Times, February 20, 2020).*

Similarly, whether it is ready-made garments, retail formats, cosmetics, building materials, construction equipment, engineering goods, all have their product and regional strongholds and compete better in certain Indian states as compared to others. Some have leadership in one product, others have leadership in others.

In India there are over 1,600 companies that are currently listed on the National Stock Exchange (NSE) and over 1,300 that are actively traded. There is no denying that many more will use the capital markets to list in due course. The fun part is that only about 200 of them would be under active coverage of institutional investors and the rest of the companies really do not get that kind of investor interest or liquidity. Illiquidity in the mid-cap space is a friend of an astute stock picker. A lack of institutional interest often means that great businesses are available at a steep discount to their intrinsic value. As the size of the economy becomes bigger, a lot of these mid-cap companies will become large cap companies and large cap companies will become ultra large market capitalisation companies, rivaling global peers.

Demographic dividend

India, in all likelihood, will be a greater than $ 5,000 per capital

GDP country in the next two decades. At that level the new businesses, industries and consumption kick the economy gets is humongous. With a relatively low cost of living, India's per capita GDP in purchasing power terms is anyway at a much higher level. Investors of our generation are truly blessed to be able to take stakes in a wide range of businesses in a well-regulated market at a time when the country is going through an inflexion. Also, as the size of the economy increases, their geo-strategic power also increases, giving them greater access to new technologies, mineral resources, talent and capital.

India's education system has continued to churn out talent in science, technology, biosciences, and a large pool of Indian-origin scientists is working across research laboratories and in technology companies worldwide. In fact, a number of very large technology companies, including Google, are headed by people of Indian origin. The importance of the Indian diaspora in the digital ecosystem will have a bearing on the growth of the digital economy going forward, as venture capital money, market focus and technologies will proliferate much faster in India, vis-à-vis a lot of other developing countries. The sheer size of the economy and the digital ecosystem make it a market impossible to ignore for the tech giants.

The diversity provides the investor an opportunity to explore his own style of investing and play in his own domain of competencies. The start-up ecosystem and fund raising is already highly evolved and exciting businesses have a pool of investors right through their growth journey to partner with. Even evolved global funds are keen to back platforms all the way from seed stage to growth stage as they keep evolving.

Similarly, real estate players with their own geographical and product strengths present a bouquet of options to participate in. REIT (real estate investment trust) has created another vehicle for real estate players to raise cheaper cost of capital and investors to participate in yield investing. InvIT presents a similar opportunity for infrastructure investors. The listed bond market is also developing and retail participation in listed NCDs and bonds has been increasing year after year.

The stock exchanges present an opportunity for those who want to play in small cap space and to those who want to play in a space with market capitalisation of over $ 10 billion. The range of industries to choose from covers the entire spectrum from technology to manufacturing and from business services to consumer facing FMCGs. Within each industry there are players who have their strengths and forte, which allows investors to choose from multiple players in the same sectors.

Leapfrogging technologies and policy interventions

Another very important aspect of India's growth has been its ability to leapfrog technologies and conventional phases of economic development. India's tele-density increased multifold with the advent of mobile phones and the majority of the country's population leapfrogged from never having had a phone to having a smartphone. Today data cost in India is one of the lowest and the penetration of smartphone is there even for the lowest strata of the population. Now the 4G penetration in the country is also pervasive and India is looking to do its 5G auctions soon. The impact of 5G spread and low data cost on the economy is likely to be further transformative.

Similarly, India also leapfrogged the general evolution of an economy that typically goes from agrarian to industrial to services. India moved from being an agrarian economy to a services economy, in many ways to circumvent the red-tape and infrastructure challenges that manufacturing brought with it. The ability to do so has created economic prosperity for a sizable population who are employed in the services industry. When the country eventually takes its rightful place in manufacturing, which it eventually will, it will not be a sweatshop for advanced countries but will have a large enough consuming population within the country as well.

The population across socio-economic segments has demonstrated amazing receptivity to technology. Farmers use it to check weather prediction and to understand best farm practices. Students can get access to information to know which are the best schools or colleges they wish to target. Access to counseling and understanding of career choices amongst today's crop of students is at a completely different level even from a decade ago. Internet has also democratised market access for the population. Anyone with a good product and a good digital marketing plan can be sitting in any part of the country and selling his produce to unlimited customers through e-commerce channels.

One does feel that the biggest benefactor of the next wave of technology will be education and healthcare services. A reliable and deep 5G network will give the country access to quality education and healthcare on a remote basis.

One of the biggest problems in the country is that the quality of healthcare in tier 3 towns and villages is absolutely abysmal, and a very large population is forced to come to cities for even secondary care requirements. Lately we are seeing a bunch of healthcare services providers looking to offer primary and secondary healthcare consultation through internet. This is not only going to reduce the pressure on healthcare delivery systems in the country but will also give access to superior healthcare to people in those towns at a fraction of the cost they would have otherwise incurred. The entire time and money spent on going to an urban center will be saved. With advancement in robotics, analytics and with the advent of 5G technology, probably even high quality tertiary care will become available on a remote basis in tier 3 towns. Possibly, India may completely leapfrog the expansion of high-cost conventional healthcare systems to a more cost-efficient and modern robotics and technology-based healthcare access.

Another bane of India's education system has been disparity in the quality of teachers in urban centers as against rural centers. A similar disparity exists between government schools and popular private schools. The difference inherently puts students from rural areas at a disadvantage while competing with urban centers. Technology in many ways is rushing in to fill in that gap. We are already seeing a proliferation of EdTech companies like BYJU'S, Vedantu, Unacademy, creating some very high quality content and delivery mechanisms. The usage of technology in classroom teaching and in test preparation space is increasing rapidly. The 5G technology will take access to live classes and quality teachers to the hinterland. The impact of some of these changes and access to technology is getting visible on a daily basis and will get more and more pronounced as we move along. The skilling and education of a large population, which hitherto looked like an impossible bridge to cross even a decade ago, may not be so difficult with modern technologies coming to the rescue.

The unlocking of potential in a country like India will be much larger than countries that already have a robust education and healthcare system. For a lot of the developed countries, these technologies will only bring down costs and replace existing infrastructure, but for India it will mean that almost half a billion people will have access to quality education and healthcare for the first time in their lives. With a robust insurance system covering 50 crore people already in place, we will hopefully bridge the gap rapidly. Seldom is a country presented with such opportunities and is at the right place to receive them. Although the pace of change may appear too slow, it will take a brave man to bet that these objectives will not be met by 2040.

India's public distribution system (PDS) has historically been a den of widespread corruption and leakages. Subsidies and welfare schemes like the rural employment scheme (MGNREGA), scholarships, fuel subsidies and other welfare programmes of the state and center have also seen large leakages. The banking inclusion programme (Jan Dhan Yojana) and direct benefit transfer plan of the government have been a roaring success, bringing a very large population into the banking channels. Leakages have been plugged and the beneficiaries now get their money directly in their bank accounts. Similarly, the UID (unique identifier) programme or Aadhaar has managed to eliminate ghost workers from government bodies, and eliminated payouts to those who don't turn up for work. At all levels these efficiencies are helping the government to spend aggressively on infrastructure while cutting leakages.

The impact of some of these programmes on its citizens has been life changing. Other social sector programmes, like making the country open defecation-free, electrification of villages and distribution of gas cylinders to over eight crore families, are changing lives in a meaningful way and allowing the population greater access to very basic facilities, more time in hand to make a living and simultaneously reducing incidence of diseases and burden on a weak healthcare system.

A country going through so many developments both on economy, social, governance front and regulatory frameworks may appear to be chaotic, and India is chaotic at the best of times. However, there is no denying that this chaotic nation does have a direction and purpose, and is surely finding its way. The solutions might be very different and probably a lot more inexpensive than what other developed nations had to pay in their journey to evolve from a mid-income economy to a high-income economy.

Stable currency and growth

The gradual currency decline coupled with import substitution and build-out of manufacturing is also creating a store of value that is inherent in the currency. This store of value is also visible in the sharp difference between India's GDP size on dollar basis and on purchasing power parity (PPP) basis. India's per capital income on PPP basis is more than twice its absolute dollar per capita income. In a world where external debt of most large democracies exceed their GDP, India with a mere 19% (FY 2019) external debt to GDP and a forex reserve exceeding half a trillion dollars, is well positioned to access both domestic and international capital for the next level of growth.

To top all that, the GDP of the country is increasing at a double digit rate year after year on a nominal basis. Although part of the reason is inflation, the relative difference in the cost of living between India and other countries means that over a period of time, inflation will only reduce the difference between dollar GDP and GDP on PPP without significantly impacting the relative foreign exchange rates. The import of this could be extremely significant for a foreign investor, as apart from gaining on the stocks he invests in, he will lose a lot lesser on the currency than he had bargained for over a longer time-frame.

Often India is seen as an expensive market to invest in vis-à-vis peers but probably in a world where governments are raising capital at close to zero yield, there is a country that presents high yields and high growth in a low-risk environment. India as a country has a track record of thousands of years of no default. The country has a large foreign exchange reserve and is aggressively eliminating primary deficit and working on import substitution. Sometimes one cannot help but feel that the global credit agencies do not upgrade India's credit rating because international investors want to continue to get these high yields in a low-risk economy.

As the relative strength of the economy keeps improving, the ability to keep India's credit rating artificially low is going to vanish, further bringing down the cost of capital for the country. Having a lower cost of capital is an extremely important thing for both the government of the day and entrepreneurs in a capital-intensive industry. A high capital cost along with a long development cycle of some projects can make the projects uncompetitive as compared to global peers even before the asset starts producing returns. Similarly, a large part of the government's budget gets spent in servicing interest and the surplus available for developmental and social sector spending gets impacted. A 2% decrease in the government's borrowing cost can release an additional INR 1,70,000 crores per year for the government for infrastructural and social sector spending, which is almost 6% of the overall budget outlay of the government.

One may have to go towards an extended period of fiscal prudence to achieve that improvement in credit rating, but the benefit that will ensue from improved ratings will create a much larger pool of capital to spend on a later date.

Rarely is a generation blessed to be able to invest in the opportunity that the Indian capital markets presents. Our economy may be low middle income but our technology platforms, payment gateways and regulatory frameworks are extremely evolved and compete with the largest economies globally. They are fully geared to cater to the next level of growth. India is at a rare juncture where each of the cycles, whether it is demography, currency or the credit cycle, can potentially play out in its favour over the next two decades. The ecosystem to capture the benefits of these positive changes is already in place. We hope this snowball of opportunities keeps gathering mass and velocity at a rapid rate, giving all stakeholders a Polycycle Bonanza!

About the Author

As a keen student of business models, Aaditya Gutgutia likes to understand the strengths and challenges facing a business from a long-term perspective. In investment banking for sixteen years, he has been heading the regional investment banking franchise of two of the largest domestic investment banks in the country for over half a decade. He believes it a privilege only a select few have, to be able to learn the nuances of different businesses from the owners of the businesses themselves.

A student of economics and of India's capital market history, he has seen the stock exchange evolve from raucous bidding on the floor of the house to terminal-based trading, with strong regulatory controls and an ever-increasing depth of foreign and domestic institutional investors. He has been a stock market investor with a prolific track record and has churned multiple ten-baggers over the last decade and a half. He has also had his share of misses and has learnt valuable lessons from those mistakes. This book captures some of his investing successes, the thought process behind the entry and exit into individual stocks and the markets in general.

This book is an effort by him to marry the discipline of investing, economics and behavioral finance to the cycles in which businesses operate. He has tried to mine his years of experience in investment banking and investing to identify new frameworks that can be of help to both amateur and professional investors. It is also an effort to capture the history of Indian capital markets and economy through an investor lens.

Aaditya has been a voracious reader of investing classics from masters like Warren Buffett, Peter Lynch, Jim Rogers and Howard Marks. The predominant bias of US investors in this domain made him aware of the need to capture the Indian capital markets with a similar kind of narrative spoken in a language best understood by the Indian capital market and examples that have a greater resonance and relevance for those who look to invest in India.

To learn more, please visit: ***www.polycycleinvestor.com***